The Administration of Justice Act 1982

with annotations by

MICHAEL J. GOODMAN, M.A., PH.D.
Solicitor

J. W. R. GRAY, M.A., LL.B.
Advocate, Lecturer in Private Law,
University of Dundee

LONDON
SWEET & MAXWELL
1983

Published in 1983 by
Sweet & Maxwell Limited of
11 New Fetter Lane, London
and printed in Great Britain
by The Eastern Press Limited
of London and Reading

ISBN 0 421 312602

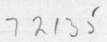

INTRODUCTION

The Administration of Justice Act 1982 has in some ways a deceptive short title. It does contain many provisions that truly concern administration of justice, in the narrower sense of the actual machinery of administration. Some of them are described below. But the more important function of the Act is the introduction of substantive law reforms in such diverse areas as damages for personal injuries, interest on all debts and damages and the validity and interpretation of wills. The Act could, in this regard, be equally described as a Law Reform (Miscellaneous Provisions) Act. Indeed, when the Bill was first introduced into the Lords, one Peer was moved to ask whether it was "intended to substitute this one measure for the entire statute book". The Lord Chancellor modestly replied by describing the Bill as a "darning exercise," likening the law to old socks that needed darning, but the Act's importance rather belies the simile. In particular, it is of first-rate importance for lawyers, their clients' activities in many vital personal fields being considerably affected. The transitional provisions of the Act will also need careful attention.

The Act's reforms are in four different areas. The first concerns the law of damages for personal injuries, including those which result in death. Loss of expectation of life as such is no longer to be the subject of compensation and the "tariff" award of e.g. £1,250 is to disappear. If diminished expectation of life causes suffering from awareness of it or loss of income for the "lost" years, then those are still proper subjects for compensation, though the latter claim is not to survive the claimant's death. The Fatal Accidents Act 1976 is amended so that a wider class of dependants can claim, including a "common-law" spouse. Moreover, a new claim for an additional fixed sum of £3,500 is introduced for the "bereavement" of a spouse or an unmarried minor child, on the death of the other spouse or parent, but this claim, too, is not to survive the death of the claimant. A profit can no longer be made by claiming damages for total loss of income at a time when the plaintiff is being maintained in a hospital, etc., at the public expense, since the saving will be set off against the loss of income claim. Rules of Court are to permit provisional awards of damages to plaintiffs who may in the future seriously deteriorate as the result of the wrongful injury, reserving a claim for further damages if this deterioration should happen. These reforms are, so far as England and Wales is concerned, to be found in Part I of the Act. There are corresponding provisions for Northern Ireland in Pt. VIII of the Act. In some respects the law of Scotland already has provisions similar to the reforms introduced by this Act but amendments, some of them similar to those for England and Wales, are made to Scottish law by Pt. II of the Act.

Secondly, the anachronistic actions in tort by a husband for loss of the services or society of his wife, by a parent for the loss of services of a child, or by a "master" for the rape, seduction or enticement of a "servant" are all abolished and, with them, the colourful case-law so beloved of generations of law students (s.2 for England and Wales; Sched. 6, para. 1 for Northern Ireland).

Thirdly, major changes are made in the law of wills by Pt. IV of the Act, applying to England and Wales, Scotland, and Northern Ireland. Because of relaxations in the formalities requisite for making wills, a purported will can no longer fail because the testator's signature is not at the "foot or end", or because a witness did not sign at the appropriate time but only acknowledged his signature, previously put there. The existing law as to revocation of wills by subsequent marriage is clarified and the possibility envisaged that a testator might want only part of his will to survive, or be revoked by, the marriage. An important reform is that divorce or annulment will normally "cut out" the former spouse from the will, whether as legatee or executor. Where a child legatee, etc., predeceases the testator and there is a saving from lapse because the child left issue surviving the testator, there will now be a "statutory transfer" of the legacy, etc., to the child's issue, instead of the artificiality of the legacy falling into the child's estate, where the principal beneficiary might have been the revenue or a trustee in bankruptcy. A relaxation of the rules forbidding extrinsic evidence to construe a will is effected by giving the court a new power to rectify a will in certain limited circumstances to make it accord with the testator's intentions. The circumstances in which, otherwise, extrinsic evidence may be admitted to explain ambiguities, etc., are also clarified. A common error, particularly in a home-made will, namely to make an absolute gift to a spouse, followed by a purported gift over to issue, will no longer give the spouse a mere life interest, and the gift to the issue will be ignored. The existing provision for depositories for the wills of living persons is reinforced by providing also for registration of such wills, including "international wills", with exchange of information between different nations. The "international will", valid as to form in all the countries signatories to the Convention, finds its place in United Kingdom law by being embodied in Sched. 2 to the Act and those authorised to do notarial acts, etc., in connection with such wills are also defined.

Fourthly, extensive new powers are conferred by Pt. III on the High Court and the county courts to award interest on debts and damages as from the date the debt, etc., accrued due, even if the debt, etc., is paid, wholly or partly, before judgment or award. Thus a claim can be made for interest alone and, although the court has a discretion (specially fettered in personal injury cases), whether or not to award interest, the possibility that now interest may be payable on any late debt may well have a considerable effect on commercial practice.

As well as these major law reforms, the Act contains, in Pt. VII, a number of minor law reforms, facilitating for example such diverse procedures as the presentation of divorce petitions by mental patients, the enforcement of orders for attachment of earnings, and the prosecution of offences under the explosives legislation.

Introduction

True "administration of justice", in its narrower sense, also finds a place in the Act. Considerable procedural amendments are made to the legislation governing the county courts and their powers and more modern provision is made for funds in any court (Pts. V and VI). The inclusion of sections relating to official referees, deputy masters of the Court of Protection, jurors, law commissioners, justices of the peace, and computers in the Land Registry perhaps justifies the statement of one Peer in debate that the Lord Chancellor's Bill was not only a very expert piece of darning but it also showed the art of darning odd socks!

A number of unsuccessful attempts were made to introduce rather more controversial provisions into the Bill. These included the enabling of solicitor Circuit Judges to become full-time High Court Judges (lost by one vote in Committee); provision as to the public disclosure of documents produced under court discovery orders (because of the controversy following the *Harman* case); and provision for High Court judges to take certain types of difficult inquests, instead of coroners. For those with an "Oxonian" bent towards "lost causes", the debates on these provisions, reported in *Hansard* (see references below) will afford fascinating reading.

MICHAEL GOODMAN

November 1982

ADMINISTRATION OF JUSTICE ACT 1982*

(1982 c. 53)

ARRANGEMENT OF SECTIONS

---

* Annotated by Michael J. Goodman, M.A., Ph.D., Solicitor and John W. R. Gray, M.A., Ll.B., Advocate, Lecturer in Private Law, University of Dundee.

PART IX

GENERAL AND SUPPLEMENTARY

An Act to make further provision with respect to the administration of justice and matters connected therewith; to amend the law relating to actions for damages for personal injuries, including injuries resulting in death, and to abolish certain actions for loss of services; to amend the law relating to wills; to make further provision with respect to funds in court, statutory deposits and schemes for the common investment of such funds and deposits and certain other funds; to amend the law relating to deductions by employers under attachment of earnings orders; to make further provision with regard to penalties that may be awarded by the Solicitors' Disciplinary Tribunal under section 47 of the Solicitors Act 1974; to make further provision for the appointment of justices of the peace in England and Wales and in relation to temporary vacancies in the membership of the Law Commission; to enable the title register kept by the Chief Land Registrar to be kept otherwise than in documentary form; and to authorise the payment of travelling, subsistence and financial loss allowances for justices of the peace in Northern Ireland.

[28th October 1982]

GENERAL NOTE

This Act was introduced as a Bill in the House of Lords by the Lord Chancellor and is described in its long title as "An Act to make further provision with respect to the administration of justice and matters connected therewith". That wide "brief" means that the Act could perhaps have been styled a Law Reform (Miscellaneous Provisions) Act, as that is essentially its character. The Bill was described by the Lord Chancellor (*Hansard*,

H.L. Vol. 428, col. 25) as "essentially a darning exercise, intended to carry out a very large number of relatively small reforms."

The major changes in the law effected by the Act (for details see below) are:

(*i*)   substantial alterations and additions to the law of damages for personal injuries (including fatal accidents) in England and Wales (Pt. I), Scotland (Pt. II), and Northern Ireland (Pt. VIII);

(*ii*) the abolition of actions in tort for loss of services of wives, children, menial servants, etc., in England and Wales (s.2) and Northern Ireland (Sched. 6, para. 1);

(*iii*) a new discretionary power for the High Court and county courts to award interest on debts and damages from the date they first became due onwards, even if they are paid (wholly or partly) before judgment (s.15);

(*iv*) reforms of the law of wills (Pt. IV), including relaxation of the formalities, provision for the effect of divorce, etc., a relaxation of the rules forbidding extrinsic evidence to construe a will, facilitation of deposit and registration of wills of living persons, and the enactment of a form of will, agreed by convention to be internationally valid, so far as form is concerned.

The other provisions of the Act are in a more minor key and include miscellaneous law reforms (Pt. VII), more modern provisions as to funds in Court (Pt. VI), provision to aid computerisation of the Land Registry (ss.66–67), and a number of provisions as to county courts, etc., which come within the more narrow meaning of "Administration of Justice" (Pt. V, ss.58–65 and 70–71).

Attempts were made to introduce a number of other changes in the law at various Parliamentary stages but they did not succeed. These included the enabling of solicitor Circuit Judges to become full-time High Court Judges (lost by one vote in committee—see now ss.58–59 of this Act); provision as to the public disclosure of documents produced under court discovery orders (because of controversy following the *Harman* case); and provision for High Court Judges to take certain types of difficult inquests, instead of coroners. For those interested in details, the *Hansard* reports of Parliamentary Debates, listed below, give full information.

Pt. I (ss.1–6) contains provisions implementing in England and Wales certain recommendations, as to the law of damages, of the Royal Commission on Civil Liability and Compensation for Personal Injury (the Pearson Commission—1978, Cmnd. 7054) and of the Law Commission (Report—1973—on Personal Injury Litigation—Assessment of Damages—Law Com. No. 56, H.C. 373): s.1 abolishes the right to damages for loss of expectation of life *per se* (though not for loss of income or diminished expectation); s.2 abolishes liability in tort for depriving a husband of the services of his wife, a parent of the services of his child, or anyone of the services of a menial or female servant; s.3 substitutes new sections 1 to 4 of the Fatal Accidents Act 1976 enlarging the scope of those dependants on behalf of whom a claim can be made, creating a new claim for £3,500 damages for bereavement for the death of a spouse or a minor unmarried child and amending the basis of assessment of damages; s.4 amends the Law Reform (Miscellaneous Provisions) Act 1934, so that claims for loss of income for "lost years" after death (see s.1) and for bereavement (see s.3) do not survive the death of the "claimant"; s.5 allows an award of damages for loss of income due to personal injuries to be reduced by the amount of financial saving to the plaintiff from being maintained at public expense in a hospital, etc; s.6 empowers the making of rules of court to provide for an award of provisional damages where there is a chance (proved or admitted) that the injured person will develop some obvious deterioration or disease, further damages in such an event to be awardable.

Pt. II (ss.7–14) contains provisions on damages for death and personal injuries under the Law of Scotland.

Pt. III (ss.15–16 and Sched. 1) gives additional power to the courts to award interest: s.15 and Sched. 1 enables the court to award interest on debt or damages from the date when the cause of action arose to the date of payment in or judgment implementing the recommendation of the Law Commission (Report No. 88, Cmnd. 7229); s.16 enables the divorce court to award interim interest on lump sum maintenance ordered to be paid at a future date.

Pt. IV by ss.17–22 implements the reports of the Law Reform Committee on the interpretation of wills 1973 (Cmnd. 5301) and on the making and revocation of wills (1980 Cmnd. 7902) *and* by ss.23–28 and Sched. 2 introduces the legislative changes necessary to enable the United Kingdom to ratify the Council of Europe Convention on the Registration of Wills, 1972 and the Unidroit (International Institute for the Unification of Private Law) Convention on the International Form of Will, 1973: s.17 contains new more liberal provisions as to the execution and witnessing of wills and repeals the existing statutory provision (Wills Act 1837, s.9); s.18 provides for the effect of a testator's subsequent marriage, divorce, etc. on his will or on gifts therein and repeals the existing statutory provision (Wills Act 1837, s.18); s.19 substitutes a new s.33 in the Wills Act 1837 providing that a gift in a will to a child or remote descendant shall not lapse if the intended beneficiary predeceases the testator leaving issue, the gift passing to those issue instead; s.20 confers power on the court to rectify a will to give effect to a testator's intentions, where it would otherwise fail to do so because of a clerical error or failure to understand the testator's intentions; s.21 allows extrinsic evidence to be admitted of for example the testator's intention to construe a will where it is ambiguous or meaningless; s.22 establishes a presumption that an apparently absolute testamentary gift to a spouse, followed by a gift to issue, gives all to the spouse and nothing to the issue; s.23 provides for the deposit and registration of wills of living persons in for example the principal registry of the family division of the High Court and s.24 designates that registry as the "national body" for the purposes of the Registration Convention of the Council of Europe; s.25 confers power to make regulations as to the deposit, registration, etc., of wills; s.26 concerns the fixing of fees for registration in Scotland; s.27 gives the force of law to the Annex to the Convention on International Wills (see above), providing a uniform law on the form of an international will, and the Annex itself is set out in Sched. 2; s.28 provides that solicitors and notaries public are authorised persons in the United Kingdom, in connection with international wills, and makes provision for the deposit, etc., of such wills.

Pt. V (ss.29–37 and Sched. 3) contains miscellaneous amendments to the law regarding county courts, as a prelude to future statutory consolidation: s.29 provides for the specification by the Lord Chancellor of county court places and districts, for example when new courts are added or old ones are closed; s.30 removes the requirement (County Courts Act 1959, s.25) that a county court registrar shall reside in the court district; s.31 gives the county court a similar power to that of the High Court in the arrest of ships, aircraft, etc., in Admiralty proceedings; s.32 enables a county court to adjudicate on a counterclaim exceeding the court's ordinary financial jurisdiction; s.33 provides for the scope of county court rules, for example in Admiralty proceedings; ss.34 and 35 provide for the enforcement in the county court of High Court judgments and orders and *vice versa*; s.36 permits the county court to adjudicate on claims for possession of mortgaged land even though there is also a money claim against a guarantor of the mortgage debt, exceeding the financial limit of the county court's jurisdiction; s.37 and Sched. 3 classify the enactments relating to the financial limits of county court jurisdiction and provide for the raising of those limits.

Pt. VI (ss.38–48) is concerned with funds paid into, held by, or paid through, a court and restates the existing statute law on the subject, with provisions uniformly applicable to the High Court and to the county court. It also confers more general powers on the Lord Chancellor and the Treasury to regulate the management and administration of funds in court: s.38 vests funds in court in the Accountant General and provides for the Administration and management of such funds; s.39 provides for the investment, etc., by the National Debt Commissioners of funds transferred to them; s.40 provides that funds deposited with the Accountant General under other legislation shall be treated as funds in court; s.41 continues provisions for the transfer of funds in court to the Official Custodian for Charities or the Church Commissioners; s.42 reproduces the Lord Chancellor's power to make common investment schemes, to enable funds in court to benefit from conglomerate investment and provides for the functioning of the Public Trustee in connection therewith; s.43 provides for the making good of any default in respect of funds in court; s.44 confers power by Order in Council to repeal or modify ss.42 and 43; s.45 provides for accounts of fund transactions; ss.46 and 47 are concerned with supplementary material and interpretation of this Part, respectively; s.48 concerns application of this Part to Scotland.

Pt. VII (ss.49–67 and Scheds. 4 and 5) contains miscellaneous law reforms: s.49 removes the restriction on the Master (and other Officers) of the Court of Protection from arranging for commencement of matrimonial proceedings on behalf of patients; s.50 empowers the Court to order maintenance to be paid by parents of a ward of court direct to the ward; s.51 gives the divorce courts further power to remit arrears of periodical payments; s.52 confines the courts' obligation to notify the Principal Registry of orders made under the Inheritance (Provision for Family and Dependants) Act 1975 to orders in respect of a deceased's estate; ss.53 and 54 amend the Attachment of Earnings Act 1971 to empower the court to order the debtor to appear before it and to specify deductions from holiday pay; s.55 and Sched. 4 enable financial institutions to deduct expenses from sums in their hands attached under garnishee orders; s.56 increases from £750 to £3,000 the maximum penalty that the Solicitors' Disciplinary Tribunal may impose on a solicitor (with power to the Lord Chancellor to adjust the maximum if there is a change in the value of money); s.57 changes the basis of requirements for the annual auditing of Judicial Trustees' accounts; ss.58–59 empowers the Lord Chancellor to request Recorders to act as High Court Judges and as Official Referees; s.60 empowers the Lord Chancellor to abolish the office of Deputy Master of the Court of Protection; s.61 permits questions as to his qualification to be put to a juror in advance of his attendance; s.62 requires a coroner to summon a jury when it is suspected that death occurred in police custody or as a result of injury by a police officer on duty; s.63 simplifies the procedure for the Attorney General giving his consent to a prosecution under the Explosives Act 1883; s.64 provides that a temporary vacancy shall not invalidate the constitution of the Law Commission; s.65 removes the existing requirement that the appointment or removal of a justice of the peace must be under the Lord Chancellor's hand; ss.66 and 67 and Sched. 5 amend the Land Registration Act 1925 to enable the register of title to be maintained other than in documentary form (for example by computer) and to clarify the county courts' jurisdiction in relation to registered land.

Pt. VIII (ss.68–72 and Scheds. 6, 7 and 8) makes various changes in the law of Northern Ireland in order to assimilate that law in certain respects to that of England and Wales; s.68 and Sched. 6 make the necessary changes in Northern Irish legislation to give effect to the same reforms in the law of damages for personal injuries as are effected for England and Wales by Pt. I of this Act; s.69 and Sched. 7 make the necessary changes in Northern Irish legislation to give effect to the enlargement of the court's powers to award interest on debts and damages, conferred in England and Wales by s.15 and Sched. 1; s.70 and Sched. 8 amend the Judicature (Northern Ireland) Act 1978, to assimilate in stated respects the position and powers of the Supreme Court of Northern Ireland to those of the Supreme Court of England and Wales; s.71 enables rules of court in Northern Ireland to provide for the disclosure of medical and other expert reports and for conditions for the giving of oral expert evidence, as is already provided by Rules of Court in England and Wales; s.72 makes provisions, similar to those in force in England and Wales, for the payment of travelling, subsistence, and financial loss allowances to justices of the peace in Northern Ireland.

Pt. IX (ss.73–78 and Sched. 9) contains general and supplementary provisions regarding commencement, transitional provisions, repeals, extent and citation: s.73 contains transitional provisions and savings; s.74 amends s.375A of the Income and Corporation Taxes Act 1970 to provide that interest awarded on damages is not subject to income tax; s.75 and Sched. 9 relate to the repeal of enactments and revocation of instruments by this Act; s.76 provides for the coming into force of this Act; s.71 specifies to what extent this Act applies to England and Wales, Scotland, and Northern Ireland respectively (see below); s.72 provides for the citation of the Act and also that the Act shall not have any effect on public funds or impose any charge on the public.

EXTENT (s.77)
England and Wales
The whole of this Act applies to England and Wales, with the exception of Pt. II (ss.7–14), ss.26 and 48, all of which apply only to Scotland *and* of Pt. VIII (ss.68–72) which applies only to Northern Ireland.
Scotland
Only Pt. II (ss.7–14), ss.23–28, 48, 7; and 75–78 of this Act apply to Scotland, Pt. II and ss.26 and 48 applying to Scotland only and not to other parts of the United Kingdom.
Northern Ireland
Ss.1, 2, 5, 64, Pt. VIII (ss.68–72) and ss.72–78 apply to Northern Ireland (except the repeal by s.75 of the Wills Act Amendment Act 1852). Part VIII (ss.68–72) applies only to Northern Ireland and not to other parts of the United Kingdom.

The repeal or amendment of a statutory provision or the revocation of an instrument by any part of this Act extends to all parts of the United Kingdom to which the statute or instrument applies, with the exception of the Wills Act Amendment Act 1852 which is not repealed for Northern Ireland (s.77(5), (6)).

COMMENCEMENT (s.76)
The complex provisions of this section are annotated in the General Note to each section of the Act, below. A considerable number of sections will not come into operation until commencement orders are made, by the Lord Chancellor, by the Secretary of State, or by them jointly. Other sections come into operation either on the day the Act was passed (October 28, 1982) or on January 1, 1983.

PARLIAMENTARY DEBATES
Hansard, H.L. Vol. 427, col. 266; Vol. 428, cols. 24, 1281; Vol. 429, cols. 163, 1105, 1290; Vol. 430, cols. 362, 422, 927; Vol. 435, col. 565; H.C. Vol. 25, col. 33; Vol. 26, col. 723; Vol. 27, col. 122; Vol. 29, col. 233.

TABLE OF EFFECTS ON EXISTING LEGISLATION
This table does not include
 (i) repeals and revocations, for which see Sched. 9;
 (ii) Scottish and Northern Irish legislation, for which see ss.3(2), 10(b) (d), 42(8), 68–72 and Scheds. 7, 8;
 (iii) purely consequential amendments in s.46 (funds in court) and Sched. III, Pt. II (county court limit).

Existing legislation (in alphabetical order)	Relevant provision of 1982 Act	Effect of 1982 Act
Administration of Justice Act 1965 (c.2). s.1(4)—common investment schemes.	s.73(8).	Gives Public Trustee power to invest in common investment funds (transitional provisions).
Administration of Justice Act 1969 (c.58). ss.22, 34(3)—award of interest by courts of record.	s.15(5).	Cease to apply to High Court and county courts.
Administration of Justice Act 1970 (c.31). s.38(1)—county court's jurisdiction where claim against mortgagor over financial limit.	s.36.	Extended to claims against guarantors.
Arbitration Act 1950 (c.27). new section 19A.	s.15(6), Sched. I, Pt. IV.	Allows arbitrator to award interest on debts, etc., paid before award.
Attachment of Earnings Act 1971 (c.32). ss.14(2), 23(1)—courts' powers in aid of attachment order.	s.53.	Gives new powers to courts to compel debtor to attend and give information as to earnings, etc.
Sched. 3, para. (4)—calculation of deductions under attachment order.	s.54.	Substitutes para. (4) allowing deduction in respect of earnings paid in advance, e.g. holiday pay.
Carriage by Railway Act 1972 (c.33). s.3(1)—restoration on actions under Fatal Accidents Act.	s.3(3).	Inserts new subsection (1A), removing restriction from action for damages for bereavement (see s.3(1) of 1982 Act).
Charging Orders Act 1979 (c.53). s.1(2)(c)—power of High Court to make charging order for over £5,000 debt.	s.34(3).	Power extended to county courts.
Commissioner for Oaths Act 1889 (c.10). s.6(1)—lists those entitled to do notarial acts abroad.	s.28(2).	Allows such persons to act in connection with international wills.

Existing legislation (in alphabetical order)	Relevant provision of 1982 Act	Effect of 1982 Act
Consular Relations Act 1968 (c.18). s.10—empowers diplomats in U.K. to do notarial acts for use abroad.	s.28(7).	Extends powers to acts *re* international wills.
Coroners (Amendment) Act 1926 (c.59). s.13(2)—requires coroner to summon jury in certain circumstances.	s.62.	Adds to circumstances, deaths in police custody or caused by police officers on duty.
County Courts Act 1959 (c.22). s.25—obliges county court registrar to reside in his district.	s.30.	Ceases to have effect.
s.57(9), (10)—provides for mode of exercise by County Court of Admiralty jurisdiction.	s.31.	New subsection (9), (10) substituted—court no longer to be satisfied, ships, etc., likely to be removed out of jurisdiction.
s.75C—transfers of counterclaims, etc., from county court to High Court, where counterclaim, etc., over financial limit.	s.32.	New s.75D inserted—gives county court jurisdiction if no transfer.
new s.97A inserted.	s.15(2), Sched. 1, Pt. II.	Gives county court power to award interest on debt., etc., paid before award.
ss.99(3), 168—moneys paid into county court.	s.73(8).	Transitional provision—rules to provide for payment to party or solicitor.
s.102(1), (3)—power to make county court rules.	s.33.	Allows rules as to Admiralty jurisdiction (see s.31) and as provided prior to January 1, 1982.
s.139—allows enforcement in county court of High Court judgments, etc.	s.34(1).	New s.139 inserted—no specific application needed.
new s.139A inserted.	s.35.	Provides for enforcement in High Court of county court judgments.
new s.143A inserted.	s.55(2), Sched. 4, Pt. II.	Allows banks, etc., to deduct expenses from sums in their hands garnisheed.
s.148—county court administration orders *re* debtors.	s.34(2).	Extends court's power to judgments of any court, *e.g.* High Court.
Courts Act 1971 (c.23). s.24(4)—Official Referees.	s.59(3).	Allows deputy circuit judges and recorders to be appointed.
Crown Proceedings Act 1947 (c.44). s.24(3)—interest on debts, damages, etc., payable by or to Crown.	s.15(3), Sched. 1, Pt. III.	Amended to include new powers to award interest—see s.15 and Sched. 1.

Existing legislation (in alphabetical order)	Relevant provision of 1982 Act	Effect of 1982 Act
Explosive Substances Act 1883. ss.7(1), 9(2)—consents to prosecutions under the 1883 Act.	s.63.	Simplifies procedure for obtaining Attorney General's *fiat*.
Family Law Reform Act 1969 (c.46). s.6(2)—High Court orders for maintenance of ward.	s.50.	Allows order for payment direct to ward.
Fatal Accidents Act 1976 (c.30). ss.1–4—set out all conditions for fatal accidents claims by dependants.	s.3.	New ss.1–4 inserted, extending classes of dependants who can claim, creating new claim for £3,500 "bereavement", and making minor and consequential amendments.
Income and Corporation Taxes Act 1970 (c.10). s.74—interest on damages for personal injuries not taxable.	s.74.	Extended to interest on all debts, etc., where interest awarded by court under new powers in s.15.
Inheritance (Provision for Family and Dependants) Act 1975 (c.63). s.19(3)—orders under Act to be filed in Family Division and memo. to be endorsed, etc., on grants of probate and administration.	s.52.	Not to apply to orders that divorced, etc., spouse not to be entitled under 1975 Act.
Judicial Trustees Act 1896. ss.1(6), 4(1)—auditing of accounts of judicial trustee.	s.57.	Amendments to ss.1(6), 4(1) and new s.4(1A) inserted—to relegate provision as to auditing of accounts to Rules to be made.
Juries Act 1974 (c.23). s.2(5)—questions to persons summoned for jury service.	s.61.	Allows questions to be submitted before attendance.
Justices of the Peace Act 1979 (c.55). s.6(1)—appointment and removal of magistrates.	s.65.	No longer required to be under *hand* of the Lord Chancellor.
Land Registration Act 1925 (c.21). new ss.1, 3(ii), 112, 113A, and 138 inserted and s.144(1) amended—keeping and inspection of registers, powers of county courts, and Rule Committee.	s.66, Sched. 5.	Provisions to facilitate computerisation of land registers, powers of county courts, and allowing Lord Chancellor to nominate Chancery Judge for Rule Committee.
Law Commissions Act 1965 (c.22). s.1(1)—constitution of Law Commission.	s.64.	Still a quorum, where below normal number by reason of temporary vacancy.

Existing legislation (in alphabetical order)	Relevant provision of 1982 Act	Effect of 1982 Act
Law Reform (Miscellaneous Provisions) Act 1934 (c.41). s.1—survival of causes of action on death.	s.4.	Not to include "bereavement" claims (see s.3) and damages for loss of income for period after death.
s.3—award of interest on judgment debts.	s.15(5).	Not to apply to High Court and county courts.
Matrimonial Causes Act 1973 (c.18). s.23—orders for financial provision in divorce, etc., proceedings.	s.16.	Interest can be awarded on deferred or instalment lump sum payments.
s.31(2)—power of High Court and county courts to vary, etc., maintenance, etc., orders.	s.51.	Power given to court to remit payment of arrears.
Mental Health Act 1959 (c.72). s.103(1)(*h*)—petitions for matrimonial relief on behalf of patients.	s.49.	Master and other Officers of Court of Protection empowered to authorise petitions.
Prevention of Fraud (Investments) Act 1958 (c.45).	s.42(8).	Not to apply to dealings or documents *re* common investment scheme.
Solicitors Act 1974 (c.47). s.47—powers of Solicitors Disciplinary Tribunal.	s.56.	Raises maximum penalty Tribunal can impose from £750 to £3,000.
Supreme Court Act 1981 (c.54). s.9(1)—persons Lord Chancellor can request to act as temporary High Court, etc., judges.	s.58.	Extended to Recorders, to act as High Court Judge.
new s.32A.	s.6.	Allows Rules of Court to permit High Court and county courts to award provisional damages for personal injuries.
new s.35A.	s.15(1), Sched. 1, Pt. I.	Gives new power to High Court to award interest on debts, etc., paid before award.
new s.40A.	s.55(1), Sched. 4, Pt. I.	Allows banks, etc., to deduct expenses from sums garnisheed in their hands.
s.68(1)—Lord Chancellor can nominate Circuit Judges as Official Referees.	s.59(1).	Extended to deputy Circuit Judges and Recorders.
s.89(6)—Lord Chancellor can abolish certain offices.	s.60.	Extended to Deputy Master of the Court of Protection.
Trustee Investments Act 1961 (c.26). Sched. 1, Pt. I—narrower range investments not requiring advice.	s.42(6).	Common investment fund deemed to be included.

Existing legislation (in alphabetical order)	Relevant provision of 1982 Act	Effect of 1982 Act
Wills Act 1837 (c.26). s.9—execution of wills.	s.17.	New section 9 substituted, no longer requiring testator's signature "at foot or end" and allowing witness to acknowledge his signature.
s.18—revocation of wills by marriage.	s.18.	New s.18 of 1837 Act substituted, replacing also s.177 of Law of Property Act 1925, and making more detailed provision for wills (or parts of wills) in contemplation of marriage.
new s.18A.	s.18.	Provides that decree of divorce, annulment, etc., revokes gifts in wills to former spouse and cancels appointment of such spouse as executor or trustee (unless contrary intention).
s.33—prevention of lapse of gifts to children, etc., who predecease testator, leaving issue surviving testator.	s.19.	New s.33 substituted, providing for direct "transfer" of such a gift to the surviving issue: gift not to fall into deceased child's estate.

PART I

DAMAGES FOR PERSONAL INJURIES ETC.

Abolition of certain claims for damages etc.

Abolition of right to damages for loss of expectation of life

1.—(1) In an action under the law of England and Wales or the law of Northern Ireland for damages for personal injuries—

(*a*) no damages shall be recoverable in respect of any loss of expectation of life caused to the injured person by the injuries; but

(*b*) if the injured person's expectation of life has been reduced by the injuries, the court, in assessing damages in respect of pain and suffering caused by the injuries, shall take account of any suffering caused or likely to be caused to him by awareness that his expectation of life has been so reduced.

(2) The reference in subsection (1)(*a*) above to damages in respect of loss of expectation of life does not include damages in respect of loss of income.

GENERAL NOTE

This section implements the recommendation of the Pearson Commission (1978, Cmnd. 7054), at paras. 363–372, that damages for loss of expectation of life as a separate head of damage should be abolished. Such damages have been assessed by the courts as a small conventional sum (see *Yorkshire Electricity Board* v. *Naylor* [1928] A.C. 529 and *Gammell* v. *Wilson* [1981] 2 W.L.R. 248,) of approximately £1,250, bearing no relation to actual losses, but acting merely as compensation for loss of happiness. The abolition was recommended because this head of damage was regarded as anachronistic. For a living plaintiff, its amount would normally be an insignificant proportion of the total damages awarded. Where the life had been terminated by death, the £1,250 sum would merely fall into the deceased's estate. There it would be a small windfall for the person(s) inheriting the estate but, if such person(s), being dependent, had a claim under the Fatal Accidents Act 1976, the sum would have to be deducted from damages recoverable under that Act. Consequently, the award usually benefited only those inheriting the estate of deceased child, where there was no dependency and therefore no Fatal Accidents Act claim. In such cases the award might well be regarded as a derisory *solatium* for, for example, a bereaved parent. In such cases, s.3 of this Act now provides for a more realistic *solatium* (see below). Where actual financial losses are caused by the shortening or termination of life, those are still remediable in damages, for example a claim for lost income (s.1(2)) or a claim for pain and suffering caused by awareness of loss of expectation of life (s.1(1)(b)).

The section comes into operation on January 1, 1983 (s.76(11)) but does not apply to causes of action which accrued before January 1, 1983 (s.73(1)). It applies only where the relevant person has died on or after January 1, 1983 (s.73(3)).

Subs. (1)(b): this subsection provides an important exception to the prohibition by subs. (1)(a) of damages for loss of expectation of life. It confirms the existing case law on the subject, which denies damages under this head to an unconscious person (see *Wise* v. *Kaye* [1962] 1 Q.B. 638, and *H. West and Son* v. *Shephard* [1964] A.C. 326). Such damages may include compensation for distress suffered by a plaintiff who realises that his dependants will be left without him to care for them (*Pickett* v. *British Rail Engineering* (1977) 121 S.J. 814, reversed by H.L. on another point, [1980] A.C. 136).

Subs. (2): this subsection provides a further important exception to the prohibition by subs. (1)(a) of damages for loss of expectation of life. Losses of income that would have been earned had expectation of life not been diminished are recoverable as damages, though reducible for the probable living expenses during the "lost years" (*Pickett* v. *British Rail Engineering* [1980] A.C. 136; *Lim* v. *Camden and Islington Area Health Authority* [1979] 2 All E.R. 910). If the plaintiff is a young child, such damages are not recoverable, as being too speculative and the damages for loss of earnings are confined to the actual, reduced, life expectation—*Croke* v. *Wiseman* [1981] 3 All E.R. 853, C.A. A claim for damages for income for the "lost years" does not survive the death of the injured person—s.4(2) of this Act, reversing on this point *Gammell* v. *Wilson* [1981] 2 W.L.R. 248.

Abolition of actions for loss of services, etc.

2. No person shall be liable in tort under the law of England and Wales or the law of Northern Ireland—

    (*a*) to a husband on the ground only of his having deprived him of the services or society of his wife;

    (*b*) to a parent (or person standing in the place of a parent) on the ground only of his having deprived him of the services of a child; or

    (*c*) on the ground only—

        (i) of having deprived another of the services of his menial servant;

        (ii) of having deprived another of the services of his female servant by raping or seducing her; or

        (iii) of enticement of a servant or harbouring a servant.

GENERAL NOTE

This section comes into operation on January 1, 1983 (s.76(11)) but does not apply to causes of action accruing before January 1, 1983 (s.73(1)).

The section implements the recommendation of the Pearson Commission (1978, Cmnd. 7054), paras. 445–447, that the actions in tort for loss of services and loss of consortium should be abolished, as being anachronistic. It must be read as a "supplement" to s.5 of the Law Reform (Miscellaneous Provisions) Act 1970 (c.33) which provided that no person was liable in tort:

    (*a*) to another person on the ground of his having induced or enticed the wife or husband of that other to leave or remain apart from that other;

    (*b*) to a parent (or person standing in the place of a parent) on the ground of his having deprived the parent (or such person) of the services of his or her child by raping, seducing, or enticing that child;

    (*c*) to another person for harbouring the wife or child of that person.

Moreover, in *Inland Revenue Commissioners* v. *Hambrook* [1956] 2 Q.B. 641, it was held that the action for loss of a servant's services applied only to "menial" servants, *i.e.* those who lived within the master's household—hence the fact, no doubt, that para. 2(*c*)(i) of this section is confined to "menial" servants.

There are, however, remedies other than the actions in tort abolished by s.5 of the 1970 Act and by this section. If the husband loses the society of his wife because of her death caused by a tort, the husband can under s.3 of this Act (adding a new s.1A to the Fatal Accidents Act 1976) claim £3,500 as damages for bereavement. An employer can indirectly recover damages from a tortfeasor who injures his employee (and thus deprives the employer of the employee's services) by placing a contractual obligation on the employee, if he recovers damages from the tortfeasor, to refund to the employer wages paid (or loaned) by the employer to the employee (see Pearson Report, paras. 502–7). Thus is circumvented the rule that there does not lie a direct action in quasi-contract for recovery of wages paid— *Receiver for Metropolitan Police District* v. *Croydon Corporation* [1957] 2 Q.B. 154.

Fatal Accidents Act 1976

Amendments of Fatal Accidents Act 1976

3.—(1) The following sections shall be substituted for sections 1 to 4 of the Fatal Accidents Act 1976—

> **"Right of action for wrongful act causing death**
>
> **1.**—(1) If death is caused by any wrongful act, neglect or default which is such as would (if death had not ensued) have entitled the person injured to maintain an action and recover damages in respect thereof, the person who would have been liable if death had not ensued shall be liable to an action for damages, notwithstanding the death of the person injured.
>
> (2) Subject to section 1A(2) below, every such action shall be for the benefit of the dependants of the person ("the deceased") whose death has been so caused.
>
> (3) In this Act "dependant" means—
>
> > (*a*) the wife or husband or former wife or husband of the deceased;
> >
> > (*b*) any person who—
> >
> > > (i) was living with the deceased in the same household immediately before the date of the death; and
> > >
> > > (ii) had been living with the deceased in the same household for at least two years before that date; and
> > >
> > > (iii) was living during the whole of that period as the husband or wife of the deceased;
> >
> > (*c*) any parent or other ascendant of the deceased;
> >
> > (*d*) any person who was treated by the deceased as his parent;
> >
> > (*e*) any child or other descendant of the deceased;
> >
> > (*f*) any person (not being a child of the deceased) who, in the case of any marriage to which the deceased was at any time a party, was treated by the deceased as a child of the family in relation to that marriage;
> >
> > (*g*) any person who is, or is the issue of, a brother, sister, uncle or aunt of the deceased.
>
> (4) The reference to the former wife or husband of the deceased in subsection (3)(*a*) above includes a reference to a person whose marriage to the deceased has been annulled or declared void as well as a person whose marriage to the deceased has been dissolved.
>
> (5) In deducing any relationship for the purposes of subsection (3) above—
>
> > (*a*) any relationship by affinity shall be treated as a relationship by consanguinity, any relationship of the half blood as a relationship of the whole blood, and the stepchild of any person as his child, and

(*b*) an illegitimate person shall be treated as the legitimate child of his mother and reputed father.

(6) Any reference in this Act to injury includes any disease and any impairment of a person's physical or mental condition.

Bereavement

1A.—(1) An action under this Act may consist of or include a claim for damages for bereavement.

(2) A claim for damages for bereavement shall only be for the benefit—

(*a*) of the wife or husband of the deceased; and

(*b*) where the deceased was a minor who was never married—

    (i) of his parents, if he was legitimate; and

    (ii) of his mother, if he was illegitimate.

(3) Subject to subsection (5) below, the sum to be awarded as damages under this section shall be £3,500.

(4) Where there is a claim for damages under this section for the benefit of both the parents of the deceased, the sum awarded shall be divided equally between them (subject to any deduction falling to be made in respect of costs not recovered from the defendant).

(5) The Lord Chancellor may by order made by statutory instrument, subject to annulment in pursuance of a resolution of either House of Parliament, amend this section by varying the sum for the time being specified in subsection (3) above.

Persons entitled to bring the action

2.—(1) The action shall be brought by and in the name of the executor or administrator of the deceased.

(2) If—

(*a*) there is no executor or administrator of the deceased, or

(*b*) no action is brought within six months after the death by and in the name of an executor or administrator of the deceased,

the action may be brought by and in the name of all or any of the persons for whose benefit an executor or administrator could have brought it.

(3) Not more than one action shall lie for and in respect of the same subject matter of complaint.

(4) The plaintiff in the action shall be required to deliver to the defendant or his solicitor full particulars of the persons for whom and on whose behalf the action is brought and of the nature of the claim in respect of which damages are sought to be recovered.

Assessment of damages

3.—(1) In the action such damages, other than damages for bereavement, may be awarded as are proportioned to the injury resulting from the death to the dependants respectively.

(2) After deducting the costs not recovered from the defendant any amount recovered otherwise than as damages for bereavement shall be divided among the dependants in such shares as may be directed.

(3) In an action under this Act where there fall to be assessed damages payable to a widow in respect of the death of her husband there shall not be taken account the re-marriage of the widow or her prospects of re-marriage.

(4) In an action under this Act where there fall to be assessed damages payable to a person who is a dependant by virtue of section 1(3)(*b*) above in respect of the death of the person with whom the dependant was living as husband or wife there shall be taken into account (together with any other matter that appears to the court to

be relevant to the action) the fact that the dependant had no enforceable right to financial support by the deceased as a result of their living together.

(5) If the dependants have incurred funeral expenses in respect of the deceased, damages may be awarded in respect of those expenses.

(6) Money paid into court in satisfaction of a cause of action under this Act may be in one sum without specifying any person's share.

Assessment of damages: disregard of benefits

4. In assessing damages in respect of a person's death in an action under this Act, benefits which have accrued or will or may accrue to any person from his estate or otherwise as a result of his death shall be disregarded.".

(2) In section 5 of the Fatal Accidents Act 1976 the words "brought for the benefit of the dependants of that person" shall be omitted.

(3) In section 3 of the Carriage by Railway Act 1972 (which provides that a person who has a right of action under that Act in respect of the death of a railway passenger shall not bring an action under the Fatal Accidents Act 1976)—

(*a*) in subsection (1)(*a*), at the beginning there shall be inserted the words "subject to subsection (1A) below,";

(*b*) the following subsection shall be inserted after that subsection—

"(1A) Nothing in subsection (1) above affects the right of any person to claim damages for bereavement under section 1A of the Fatal Accidents Act 1976."; and

(*c*) in subsection (4), after the word "Order", in the second place where it occurs, there shall be inserted the words ", the reference to section 1A of the Fatal Accidents Act 1976 in subsection (1A) above shall be construed as a reference to Article 3A of that Order".

GENERAL NOTE

This section implements some, but not all, of the recommendations of the Pearson Commission (1978, Cmnd. 7054), paras. 399–431 as to claims under the Fatal Accidents Act 1976 ("dependency" claims). It does so by repealing the original ss.1–4 of the 1976 Act, substituting new ss.1, 1A, 2, 3, and in that Act, and by making consequential amendments to s.5 of the 1976 Act and to s.3 of the Carriage by Railway Act 1972—for the changes in the law see below. This section comes into force on January 1, 1983 (s.76(11)) and does not apply to causes of action accruing before that date (s.73(1)).

Subs. (1): this subsection repeals the original s.1–4 of the Fatal Accidents Act 1976 (c.30), substituting in that Act new ss.1, 1A, 2, 3, and 4. Each of those new sections is annotated below:—

S.1(1)

This subsection is identical to the original section 1(1) of the Fatal Accidents Act 1976.

S.1(2)

Apart from the words, "Subject to section 1A(2) below" (referring to the new claim for damages for bereavement), this subsection is identical to the original s.1(2) of the Fatal Accidents Act 1976.

S.1(3)

This subsection amends the law of England and Wales as to those dependants entitled to claim to bring it into line with the law in Scotland (now contained in Sched. 1 to the Damages (Scotland) Act 1976 (c.13)). It enlarges the classes of dependants entitled to claim (provided there is financial dependency) in the following respects:

(*i*) as well as the deceased's spouse, a former spouse can claim (new s.1(3)(*a*)), whether the former marriage terminated by divorce or decree of nullity (new s.1(5)). Moreover, a claim can also be made by a person not married to the deceased but living in the same household with him (her) as spouse at the death and for at least two years prior to that date (sometimes referred to as a "common-law" husband or wife). Such a person's damages must, however, take into account the fact that the common-law spouse had as such no enforceable right to financial support (new s.3(4)).

(ii) *any* ascendant or descendant of the deceased, no matter how remote (and not merely parent, grandparent, child, and grandchild, as hitherto) can claim (new s.1(3)(*c*) and (*e*)).

(iii) a person not the deceased's parent or child, but treated by him (her) as such can claim (new s.1(3)(*d*) and (*f*)), though, in the case of a "child" only if he or she were treated by the deceased as a child in the sense of a child of the family in relation to any marriage of the deceased (s.1(3)(*f*)).

The remaining categories of dependant in the new s.1(3) of the 1976 Act, for example, brother, cousin, uncle, are the same as in the original s.1(3).

S.1(4)

See annotation (i) to s.1(3), above.

S.1(5)

This subsection is identical to the original s.1(4) of the Fatal Accidents Act 1976. Relationship by affinity means by marriage and by consanguinity means by blood. Adoptive relationships (parent and child) are included by virtue of the Children Act 1975 (c.72), Sched. 1.

S.1(6)

This subsection is identical to the original s.1(5) of the Fatal Accidents Act 1976.

S.1A

This section is entirely new and follows the limited recommendations of the 1973 Report of the Law Commission (Law Com. No. 56, H.C. 373) rather than the broader recommendations, for "loss of society" awards, of the Pearson Commission (1978, Cmnd. 7054). It introduces a new claim for damages for bereavement of £3,500 (not an upper limit, but a fixed figure to be awarded in all cases). That figure can be varied by Order of the Lord Chancellor (s.1(5)).

The only persons entitled to claim such damages are (i) a spouse of the deceased; (ii) the father (only if child legitimate) and mother of a deceased minor child who was never married (new s.1(2)). The claim is in addition to any claim for lost financial support, though such a claim is unlikely in case (ii). The new claim for bereavement will in some cases supersede the former inherited claim for loss of expectation of life, now abolished by s. 1(1)(*a*) of this (1982) Act (see above).

S.2

This section is identical to the original s.2 of the Fatal Accidents Act 1976, except that references to "dependants" have been deleted, in view of the wider classification of claimants introduced by the new s.1(3)—see above. The change is purely consequential and of itself makes no alteration in the law.

S.3

Apart from subs. (4) which is new (see below), this section is (subject to minor changes in wording, not altering the law) identical to the original s.3 of the Fatal Accidents Act 1976.

Subs. (4) relates to the new right to claim of a "common-law" spouse—see the note to the new s.1(3) above and requires the court, in assessing damages, to take into account the fact that the "spouse" had no enforceable right to financial support by the deceased as the result of their living together. In debate, the Lord Chancellor stated that the provision was to "make clear to the court that one of the factors which it ought to take into account in applying the durability test, in applying the multiplicator, was that the relationship was one which could be determined by the will of either party without legal proceedings and without giving rise to an obligation on the part of the other". It was not intended to give rise to merely token awards. (*Hansard*, H.L. Vol. 429, col. 1108).

S.4

This section is new and implements a recommendation of the Pearson Commission (1978, Cmnd. 7054), paras. 537–539. Fatal Accidents Act 1976 exempted from deduction from damages under the Act only insurance moneys, certain benefits, pensions or gratuities paid, etc., as a result of the death. All other gains to a dependant as a result of the death, for example, damages for the deceased's pain and suffering inherited as part of the deceased's state, had to be deducted from the damages under the 1976 Act. Now, under the new section 4, no benefits of any kind are to be deducted from such damages, whether inherited from the deceased's estate or in any other way accruing as a result of the death, for example by right of survivorship in a joint tenancy of real or personal property.

Subs. (2): This merely makes a consequential amendment to s.5 of the Fatal Accidents Act 1976 (providing for reduction of damages for the deceased's contributory negligence), as a result of the enlargement by the new s.1(3) of the 1976 Act of the classes of those entitled to claim, who may not all be truly called "dependants", though they must still have suffered financial loss for a claim to succeed.

Subs. (3): S.3(1) of the Carriage by Railway Act 1972 (c.33), coupled with Sched. 1, art. 3 (para. 2) of that Act, provides that no action can be maintained under the Fatal Accidents Act 1976 in respect of the death of a passenger by persons towards whom the passenger had, or would have had in the future, *a legally enforceable duty to maintain,* such persons having to found their claim on the provisions of the 1972 Act.

Subs. (3) of this (1982) Act amends the 1972 Act so as to enable such persons nevertheless to make a claim for damages for bereavement under the new section 1A of the Fatal Accidents Act 1976, introduced by subs. (1)—see above. A consequential amendment is made to the Fatal Accidents Order in Northern Ireland (S.I. 1977 No. 1251).

Claims not surviving death

Exclusion of Law Reform (Miscellaneous Provisions) Act 1934

4.—(1) The following subsection shall be inserted after section 1(1) of the Law Reform (Miscellaneous Provisions) Act 1934 (actions to survive death)—

> "(1A) The right of a person to claim under section 1A of the Fatal Accidents Act 1976 (bereavement) shall not survive for the benefit of his estate on his death.".

(2) The following paragraph shall be substituted for subsection (2)(*a*)—

> "(*a*) shall not include—
> > (i) any exemplary damages;
> > (ii) any damages for loss of income in respect of any period after that person's death;".

GENERAL NOTE

This section makes two exclusions from the survival on the death of a "plaintiff" of a cause of action vested in him (her). Such survival was enacted by s.1 of the Law Reform (Miscellaneous Provisions) Act 1934 (c.41) as an exception to the common law rule that a personal action dies with the person (*actio personalis moritur cum persona*) and that rule still applies to causes of action excluded from s.1 of the 1934 Act. The two exclusions effected by this section and thus dying with the "plaintiff" are (i) the new claim for damages for bereavement introduced by s.3 of this Act (see above); (ii) a claim for damages for loss of income or earnings for the "lost years" when a "plaintiff's" life expectation has been diminished by the tort. This section comes into force on January 1, 1983 (s.76(11)) and does not apply to causes of action accruing before that date (s.73(1)). (See also the note to subs. (2) below.)

Subs. (1): The exclusion from survival on death of the new claim for damages for bereavement follows the recommendation of the Pearson Commission (1978, Cmnd. 7054), paras. 440–441. Damages for pain, suffering, and loss of amenity will, however, continue to be claimable after death and will fall into the deceased's estate (as recommended by the Pearson Commission (paras. 442–444)).

Subs. (2): this subsection applies only to a death on or after January 1, 1983 (s.70(3),(4)). The amended s.1(2)(*a*) of the Law Reform (Miscellaneous Provisions) Act 1934 thus reads:

> "1 (2) Where a cause of action survives . . . for the benefit of the estate of a deceased person, the damages recoverable for the benefit of the estate of that person:—
> > (*a*) shall not include—
> > > (i) any exemplary damages;
> > > (ii) any damages for loss of income in respect of any period of that person's death;".

(Only s.1(2)(*a*)(ii) is new.)

The exclusion from survival on death of a claim for damages for loss of income or earnings for the "lost years" when a "plaintiff's" life expectation has been diminished was recommended by the Pearson Commission (Cmnd. 7054), on the ground of duplication of damages where there were Fatal Accident Act claims, but the House of Lords felt constrained to decide otherwise in *Gammell* v. *Wilson* [1981] 2 W.L.R. 248, H.L. See also *Benson* v. *Biggs Wall & Co.* [1982] 3 All E.R. 300; *Harris* v. *Empress Motors* [1982] 3 All E.R. 306; and *Clay* v. *Pooler* [1982] 3 All E.R. 570. *Gammell* v. *Wilson* is now reversed by this section. However, a claim for loss of earnings between the dates of the tort and of the death of the injured person (when a time interval separates them) will continue to survive the death. Moreover, a live plaintiff can still claim damages for loss of earnings for the "lost years"— see *Pickett* v. *British Rail Engineering* [1980] A.C. 136.

Maintenance at public expense

Maintenance at public expense to be taken into account in assessment of damages

5. In an action under the law of England and Wales or the law of Northern Ireland for damages for personal injuries (including any such action arising out of a contract) any saving to the injured person which is attributable to his maintenance wholly or partly at public expense in a hospital, nursing home or other institution shall be set off against any income lost by him as a result of his injuries.

GENERAL NOTE

This section implements a recommendation of the Pearson Commission (1978, Cmnd. 7054), paras. 508–512 that the value of maintenance provided by a public authority should be taken into account in the assessment of damages. This section (reversing *Daish* v. *Wauton* [1972] 1 Q.B. 262, C.A.) imposes this offset but confines it to damages for loss of income. If, however, a plaintiff chooses to seek private medical, etc., treatment, instead of that available through the National Health Service, he can claim damages for the fees, for example of a private nursing home, even though precisely the same facilities are available through the N.H.S.—Law Reform (Personal Injuries) Act 1948, s.2(4). The Pearson Commission's recommendation that a requirement of reasonableness should be superimposed (paras. 339–342) has not been implemented in this Act. However, the saving in such cases of board and lodging costs may be deductible from damages (*Shearman* v. *Folland* [1950] 2 K.B. 43, C.A.). This section comes into operation on January 1, 1983 (s.76(11)) and does not apply to causes of action accruing before that date (s.78(1)).

Provisional damages for personal injuries

Award of provisional damages for personal injuries

6.—(1) The following section shall be inserted after section 32 of the Supreme Court Act 1981—

"Orders for provisional damages for personal injuries

32A.—(1) This section applies to an action for damages for personal injuries in which there is proved or admitted to be a chance that at some definite or indefinite time in the future the injured person will, as a result of the act or omission which gave rise to the cause of action, develop some serious disease or suffer some serious deterioration in his physical or mental condition.

(2) Subject to subsection (4) below, as regards any action for damages to which this section applies in which a judgment is given in the High Court, provision may be made by rules of court for enabling the court, in such circumstances as may be prescribed, to award the injured person—

(*a*) damages assessed on the assumption that the injured person will not develop the disease or suffer the deterioration in his condition; and

(*b*) further damages at a future date if he develops the disease or suffers the deterioration.

(3) Any rules made by virtue of this section may include such incidental, supplementary and consequential provisions as the rule-making authority may consider necessary or expedient.

(4) Nothing in this section shall be construed—

(*a*) as affecting the exercise of any power relating to costs, including any power to make rules of court relating to costs; or (*b*) as prejudicing any duty of the court under any enactment or rule of law to reduce or limit the total damages which would have been recoverable apart from any such duty.".

(2) In section 35 of that Act (supplementary) "32A," shall be inserted before "33" in subsection (5).

(3) The section inserted as section 32A of the Supreme Court Act 1981 by subsection (1) above shall have effect in relation to county courts as it has effect in relation to the High Court, as if references in it to rules of court included references to county court rules.

GENERAL NOTE

This section introduces a new s.32A into the Supreme Court Act 1981, after s.32 (which concerns interim payments of damages). The section will not come into force until a commencement order is made by the Lord Chancellor (s.76(1) and (2)) but will then apply to actions whenever commenced, even before the passing of this Act (s.73(2)). New Rules of the Supreme Court and County Court Rules will be needed to give substance to the section.

The section implements with variations the recommendations of the Law Commission's Report (1973) (Personal Injury Litigation—Assessment of Damages; Law Com. No. 56, H.C. 373) and of the Pearson Commission (1978, Cmnd. 7054), paras. 584–585, though the recommendation of both bodies that provisional awards should be made only where the defendant was a public authority or was insured in respect of the plaintiff's claim has not been adopted.

The Lord Chancellor, introducing the Bill in the House of Lords (*Hansard,* H.L. Vol. 428, cols. 28–29) stated that what was proposed was "that the courts should be empowered to make a provisional award in cases where the medical prognosis is particularly uncertain and where there is a chance, falling short of probability, that some serious disease or serious deterioration in the plaintiff's condition will accrue at a later date . . . The purpose [of this section] is to make it possible for the court to take a different approach, to wait and see; that is, to award nothing in respect of the feared event but to give damages for what is known, and then to allow the plaintiff to apply for damages later if the feared event actually takes place. In all other respects, the award is, of course, perfectly normal. I do not imagine that this procedure will be employed very often. It will not be involved unless the plaintiff wants it and the court is satisfied that this procedure will not cause serious prejudice to the defendant." This was to be contrasted with the existing procedure by which the courts award some damages for the feared event, but much reduced for the contingency that that event (for example a possibility of epilepsy following a skull fracture) might not occur.

Subs. (1). This subsection introduces a new s.32A into the Supreme Court Act 1981 (as to the coming into force and the general effect of the new section: see General Note above). "Personal injuries" in the new section include "any disease and any impairment of a person's physical or mental condition" (1981 Act, s.35(5), as amended by s.6(2) of this Act). Subs. (4)(*b*) of the new s.32A makes the new provisional awards subject to (i) overall limits for damages under statutes, etc., for example Carriage by Railway Act 1972, Sched., Art. 6 or the financial limit of County Court jurisdiction (*cf.* ss.6(3), and 37 of this Act); (ii) reduction of damages for contributory negligence under the Law Reform (Contributory Negligence) Act 1945.

Subs. (2): This has the effect of defining "personal injuries" in the new s.32A of the 1981 Act—see the note to subs. (1) above.

Subs.(3): Provisional awards will be possible in the county court subject to (i) the making of the necessary county court rules; (ii) the overall financial limit of jurisdiction (new s.32A(4)(*b*)), as to which, see the General Note to s.37 below.

PART II

DAMAGES FOR PERSONAL INJURIES, ETC.—SCOTLAND

GENERAL NOTE

Apart from certain amendments, ss.7 to 10 and s.13 follow almost entirely cll. 1 to 5 of a draft of a Damages (Scotland) Bill proposed by the Scottish Law Commission (Scot. Law Com. No. 51 (1978)). There, the recommendations relating to claims for services and admissible deductions of the Royal Commission on Civil Liability and Compensation for

Personal Injury, the Pearson Commission, (Cmnd. 7054) were considered. However, any modifications suggested by the Scottish Law Commission have been preferred in ss.8 to 10. Ss.11 and 12, by contrast, follow directly from recommendations of the Pearson Commission, the provisions of s.11 replicating those of s.5 in Part I, though s.12 was amended in the House of Lords at the report stage after the views of the Lord President of the Court of Session had been sought. S.14 puts into effect a recommendation of the Scottish Law Commission (Scot. Law Com. No. 64 (1981)).

The contents of Pt. I, which extend to other parts of the United Kingdom, and Pt. II differ considerably because of the improvements effected for Scotland in the Damages (Scotland) Act 1976. With the exceptions of ss.12 and 14(2), Pt. II came into force on January 1, 1983—s.76(11).

Damages in respect of services

7. Where a person (in this Part of this Act referred to as "the injured person")—

(*a*) has sustained personal injuries, or

(*b*) has died in consequence of personal injuries sustained,

as a result of an act or omission of another person giving rise to liability in any person (in this Part of this Act referred to as "the responsible person") to pay damages, the responsible person shall also be liable to pay damages in accordance with the provisions of sections 8 and 9 of this Act.

GENERAL NOTE

This preliminary section outlines in broad terms the circumstances where Pt. II applies, namely personal injuries or death resulting from such. The "injured person" is the party to whom liability is incurred while the "responsible person" is the person who incurs liability. "Personal injuries" are given an extended definition in s.13(1). This terminology is used throughout the Act.

Services rendered to injured person

8.—(1) Where necessary services have been rendered to the injured person by a relative in consequence of the injuries in question, then, unless the relative has expressly agreed in the knowledge that an action for damages has been raised or is in contemplation that no payment should be made in respect of those services, the responsible person shall be liable to pay to the injured person by way of damages such sum as represents reasonable remuneration for those services and repayment of reasonable expenses incurred in connection therewith.

(2) The relative shall have no direct right of action in delict against the responsible person in respect of the services or expenses referred to in this section, but the injured person shall be under an obligation to account to the relative for any damages recovered from the responsible person under this section.

GENERAL NOTE

Subs. (1): The subsection grants the injured person a right to recover damages from the responsible person to allow reasonable remuneration of a relative providing the injured person, in consequence of his injuries, with necessary services and also to defray the relative's expenses. Until the Act came into operation, such damages could be obtained only where there had been actual remuneration of another by the injured person or defrayment of his expenses or an obligation to do either of these had been incurred. It is, however, only where the person rendering the services is a relative (defined in s.13(1)) that the provision operates. This is contrary to the position taken both by the English Law Commission (Law Com. No. 56 (1973)) and the Pearson Commission. Whether the claim should be so restricted must remain doubtful. The relatives defined in the Act are the same as those entitled to sue for loss of support on the death of an injured person in terms of s.1 of the Damages (Scotland) Act 1976. Where the relative has expressly agreed that no payment should be made, damages are not, however, payable. This agreement may be either oral or written and take place at any time after the accident, the onus being on the responsible person to establish it. The mere fact that the relative undertook the services without thought of payment is immaterial and no question arises as to the relative having tacitly waived any right to payment. Moreover, the agreement must be made in the knowledge that an action for damages has either been raised by the injured person or is in contemplation by him. This provision, one of a number of amendments proposed by Mr. Donald Dewar, M.P. at the report stage in the House of Commons which was accepted by the Solicitor-General for Scotland, is "an attempt to establish that the specific agreement that no compensation shall be received by the relative should be made at a time when the relative had knowledge that there was a possibility of recovery by an action for damages" (see H.C. (October 19, 1982), col. 286: Mr. Donald Dewar).

The recommendation (3) of the Scottish Law Commission (para. 27) was that the expression "necessary services" should not be defined, the term "necessary" being self-explanatory, the ordinary test of reasonableness and the ordinary requirement of minimisation of loss being applicable to the determination of a claim, which should not be restricted to services of an extraordinary nature, services such as nursing and attendance being chiefly envisaged (para. 25). The Commission also recommend (para. 26) that the amount of damages should not necessarily be calculated on the basis of the relative's loss of earnings (if any) but rather of what in the particular case would be reasonable together with repayment of incidental expenses—see explanatory note to cl. 2 of their draft Bill.

On the death of the injured person, the right to claim damages for the period to the date of death falls to his executor by virtue of s.2(1) of the Damages (Scotland) Act 1976.

Subs. (2): The subsection ensures that the responsible person is confronted by only one action in respect of such services unless there is, for example, a direct agreement between the person performing the services and himself. At common law, it was doubtful whether relatives had a direct right of action in respect of services to the injured person though in *McBay* v. *Hamlett* 1963 S.C. 282, it was held that the latter's husband had a relevant claim in respect of visits to his wife in hospital and employing a housekeeper. This case is now overruled.

It is provided that the injured person must account to the relative for the damages recovered but only for the actual sum received since these will be reduced where there is contributory negligence and may be when there is a settlement or a statutory limitation on the amount.

Services to injured person's relative

9.—(1) The responsible person shall be liable to pay to the injured person a reasonable sum by way of damages in respect of the inability of the injured person to render the personal services referred to in subsection (3) below.

(2) Where the injured person has died, any relative of his entitled to damages in respect of loss of support under section 1(3) of the Damages (Scotland) Act 1976 shall be entitled to include as a head of damage under that section a reasonable sum in respect of the loss to him of the personal services mentioned in subsection (3) below.

(3) The personal services referred to in subsections (1) and (2) above are personal services—

    (*a*) which were or might have been expected to have been rendered by the injured person before the occurrence of the act or omission giving rise to liability,

    (*b*) of a kind which, when rendered by a person other than a relative, would ordinarily be obtainable on payment, and

    (*c*) which the injured person but for the injuries in question might have been expected to render gratuitously to a relative.

(4) Subject to subsection (2) above, the relative shall have no direct right of action in delict against the responsible person in respect of the personal services mentioned in subsection (3) above.

GENERAL NOTE

Subs. (1): The subsection, as the rubric, at least, makes clear, deals with services to a relative (defined in s.13(1)). The subsection marks a notable departure from the ordinary principles of delict in Scots law whereby the pursuer must first have sustained loss. It states that if an injured person is no longer able to give personal services (defined in subs. (3)), the injured person himself should receive compensation, and the injured person alone. The purpose again is to avoid a multiplicity of actions.

On the death of the injured person, the right to claim damages for the period to the date of death falls to his executor by virtue of s.2(1) of the Damages (Scotland) Act 1976.

Subs. (2): The subsection makes express provision for the situation where the injured person's death supervenes. Once again, multiplicity of actions is avoided by treating the relative's claim as one for loss of support.

Subs. (3): The subsection outlines the nature of the personal services: (a) They must have been rendered or were expected to have been rendered prior to the delictual event; (b) when not performed by a relative would ordinarily have been paid for; and (c) the injured person might have been expected to render them gratuitously.

The loss must not be merely of a non-patrimonial nature as in a loss of society award in terms of s.1(4) of the 1976 Act. The Scottish Law Commission (Scot. Law Com. No. 51 (1978) para. 39) decided against awards of the latter kind being included mainly because a loss of society award is based on the consideration that the deceased's family lose the benefit of the counsel and guidance expected of him while he remained alive and accordingly takes his death for granted.

Subs. (4): Under the terms of the subsection, no claim for damages in delict by the relative is competent against the responsible person in respect of the services except as provided for in subs. (2). Other claims for loss of services are not specifically excluded though it would appear that these are not recognised at common law (see Walker: "The Law of Delict in Scotland" (2nd edit. revised) W. Green & Son, Edinburgh, 1981, pp. 916–917).

Assessment of damages for personal injuries

10. Subject to any agreement to the contrary, in assessing the amount of damages payable to the injured person in respect of personal injuries there shall not be taken into account so as to reduce that amount—

(*a*) any contractual pension or benefit (including any payment by a friendly society or trade union);

(*b*) any pension or retirement benefit payable from public funds other than any pension or benefit to which section 2(1) of the Law Reform (Personal Injuries) Act 1948 applies;

(*c*) any benefit payable from public funds, in respect of any period after the date of the award of damages, designed to secure to the injured person or any relative of his a minimum level of subsistence;

(*d*) any redundancy payment under the Employment Protection (Consolidation) Act 1978, or any payment made in circumstances corresponding to those in which a right to a redundancy payment would have accrued if section 81 of that Act had applied;

(*e*) any payment made to the injured person or to any relative of his by the injured person's employer following upon the injuries in question where the recipient is under an obligation to reimburse the employer in the event of damages being recovered in respect of those injuries;

(*f*) subject to paragraph (iv) below, any payment of a benevolent character made to the injured person or to any relative of his by any person following upon the injuries in question;

but there shall be taken into account—

(i) any remuneration or earnings from employment;

(ii) any unemployment benefit;

(iii) any benefit referred to in paragraph (*c*) above payable in respect of any period prior to the date of the award of damages;

(iv) any payment of a benevolent character made to the injured person or to any relative of his by the responsible person following on the injuries in question, where such a payment is made directly and not through a trust or other fund from which the injured person or his relatives have benefited or may benefit.

GENERAL NOTE

The section sets out the various payments which are not to be taken into account in assessing damages at (*a*) to (*f*).

Payments which are to be taken into account are listed at (i) to (iv). The parties are free to vary the provisions set out in the section, the latter moreover applying only to actions at the instance of the injured person himself or his executor and not to actions for loss of support covered by s.1(5) of the Damages (Scotland) Act 1976.

(*a*) is the equivalent of s.1(5)(*b*) of the 1976 Act which deals with the rights of the relatives in claims for loss of support. In the equivalent cl. (4) of their draft Bill, the Scottish Law Commission specifically included payment under an insurance policy and in their recommendation (para. 72) referred to pensions arising from employment, where the benefit may be provided by the defender. However, they point out (para. 71) that specific provision may be made in the scheme for this contingency.

(*b*) relates to payment from public funds. This expression remains undefined but this is of no consequence in view of the provisions under (*a*) and (*f*) (the latter relating to payments of a benevolent character) in the opinion of the Scottish Law Commission in their explanatory note to the equivalent clause in their draft Bill. The provision is certainly wide enough in its terms to cover existing or future benefits payable on retirement by the state or a public authority regardless of whether the injured person is an employee. However, sickness benefit, invalidity benefit, non-contributory invalidity pension, injury benefit and disablement benefit being listed in s.2(1) (as amended) of the Law Reform (Personal Injuries) Act 1948 will be subject to a 50 per cent. deduction over a five-year period from the time when the cause of action accrued (see Walker: "The Law of Delict in Scotland," p. 474). The exclusion of the pensions or benefits referred to from the full effect of the provision (if the particular limitations of the 1948 Act are met) is the result of an amendment introduced at the report stage in the House of Commons to ensure that the United Kingdom social security benefits receive even-handed treatment throughout the United Kingdom (see *Hansard*, H.C. (October 19, 1982), col. 293).

(*c*), by contrast, makes express reference to payments to relatives as well as to the injured person himself from public funds to secure a minimum level of subsistence. Benefit relating to any period up to the date of the award will be taken into account in assessing damages but not otherwise—s.10(iii). This is in line with the recommendation of the Pearson Commission (para. 494), who point out that, after the award, the injured person will have his damages, which will be taken into account in deciding on eligibility for supplementary benefit or family income supplement. By contrast, such payments made prior to the award diminish the loss and should be deducted.

At the committee stage in the House of Commons, the Solicitor-General for Scotland pointed out that (*c*) would cover payments such as supplementary benefit or other means-tested benefit like family supplement, its aim being to make clear that the right to these benefits is to be excluded in making the assessment because their purpose is to provide subsistence for persons whose income from all sources is insufficient for their needs (see H.C. Standing Committee A (July 6, 1982), col. 24). He emphasised that the explicit reference made to payments to relatives ensures that damages claimed for loss of earnings will not be modified because of the possibility of supplementary benefit being payable (*ibid.* col. 25). The benefits have been deliberately left unspecified as these change with time.

(*d*) relates to redundancy payments made by an employer to an injured person in his employment on the termination of his services as well as other payments made in corresponding circumstances.

(*e*) relates to payments made to the injured person or a relative by the employer of the former after the injuries have been sustained while there is an obligation of reimbursement on damages being recovered. This provision, similar to the recommendation of the Pearson Commission (para. 505), confirms the position at common law—see *Doonan* v. *S.M.T. Co.* 1950 S.C. 136, where the injured party continued to receive from her employer her wages as housekeeper, though incapacitated, after being injured in a road accident, on the understanding that if damages were recovered, the wages would be repaid. It was held that, in assessing the amount of damages, the jury were entitled to take the obligation of repayment into account.

(*f*) follows the position at common law, where there is English and Northern Irish, as well as Scottish, authority to the effect that benevolent payments to an injured person or his relatives are not to be taken into account in assessing damages, at least as a general rule, such to include benevolent payments from an employer unless (see (iv)) he is also the responsible person—see *Liffen* v. *Watson* [1940] 1 K.B. 556; *Peacock* v. *Amusement Equipment Co.* [1954] 2 All E.R. 689, dicta in *Parry* v. *Cleaver* [1970] A.C. 1, also dictum in *Browning* v. *The War Office* [1963] 1 Q.B. 750 at p.759; *Redpath* v. *Belfast and County*

Down Railway Co. [1947] N.I. 167 and *Dougan* v. *Rangers F.C.* 1974 S.L.T.(Sh.Ct.) 34. Payments from an employer not coming under the provisions of (*e*) and (*f*) would fall to be deducted as the injured person could not then be considered as having lost this amount in earnings.

(i) to (iv) list payments to be taken into account in assessing damages.

(i) asserts the common-law principle to be found in *Metropolitan Police District Receiver* v. *Croydon Corporation*; *Monmouthshire C.C.* v. *Smith* [1957] 2 Q.B. 154 that, generally speaking, earnings from employment are to be deducted from the amount of damages, since the loss is diminished, (*e*) providing an exception as does (*f*) where the payment is of a benevolent character.

(ii) confirms the decisions of *McPherson* v. *Kelsey Roofing Industries* 1967 S.L.T. (Notes) 93 and *Gallagher* v. *I.C.I.* 1970 S.L.T. (Notes) 41. The English Law Commission (Law Com. No. 56 (1973) para. 136–7) took the view that unemployment benefit should no longer be taken into account in personal injuries cases on the ground that there was an analogy with pensions. By contrast, the Scottish Law Commission (Scot. Law Com. No. 51 (1978) para. 96) regarded unemployment benefit as a species of surrogatum offered by the state's social security scheme for loss of earnings while there is also a direct causal connection between the earnings lost and the benefit received, a factor not present in the case of other social security benefits. The Pearson Commission (para. 492) reached a similar conclusion though they felt the question would, in practice, arise infrequently since the benefit is payable only when the claimant is fit to work.

(iii) implements, in part, the recommendation of the Scottish Law Commission (*op. cit.* para. 80) who, in turn, were influenced by the views of the Pearson Commission (para. 494) referred to above in relation to (*c*).

(iv) embodies an exception to the general rule that benevolent payments are not to be taken into account in assessing damages, an exception applying solely to payments to the injured person or his relatives by the responsible person or on his behalf, whether or not he is also the employer.

It was made clear by the Solicitor-General for Scotland at the report stage in the House of Commons that the purpose of taking the latter into account was to encourage payments to be made by the responsible person in advance of a court action (see *Hansard*, H.C. (October 19, 1982), col. 290). Unlike the position in the draft Bill of the Scottish Law Commission, where it was a matter of implication, it is specifically provided that the payment must be made directly and not through a trust or other fund. The Pearson Commission (para. 536) made a similar recommendation where they specified that if the payments are to be taken into account they must not be contributions to a general fund from which people other than the plaintiff also benefit. (The Act makes no such qualification though it seems unlikely that this will make much difference in practice.) This provision marks no deviation from the common law. In *Dougan* v. *Rangers F.C.*, the children of a person killed in an accident at a football ground were able to have payments made from a disaster fund excluded even though the defenders had contributed.

Maintenance at public expense to be taken into account in assessment of damages: Scotland

11. In an action for damages for personal injuries (including any such action arising out of a contract) any saving to the injured person which is attributable to his maintenance wholly or partly at public expense in a hospital, nursing home or other institution shall be set off against any income lost by him as a result of the injuries.

GENERAL NOTE

The section replicates the provisions of s.5 of Pt. I providing that maintenance at public expense will be taken into account in assessing damages. It follows a recommendation of the Pearson Commission (para. 512) to the effect that the value of maintenance provided by a public authority should be taken into account. Accordingly, the English case of *Daish* v. *Wauton* [1972] 2 Q.B. 262, a decision of the Court of Appeal, is now reversed.

At the report stage in the House of Commons, the Solicitor-General of Scotland pointed out that there is no question of offsetting the full cost of the maintenance but merely that element of the injured person's living expenses he no longer has to meet while he is being cared for in a public institution (see *Hansard*, H.C. (October 19, 1982), col. 291).

Award of provisional damages for personal injuries: Scotland

12.—(1) This section applies to an action for damages for personal injuries in which—

(a) there is proved or admitted to be a risk that at some definite or indefinite time in the future the injured person will, as a result of the act or omission which gave rise to the cause of the action, develop some serious disease or suffer some serious deterioration in his physical or mental condition; and

(b) the responsible person was, at the time of the act or omission giving rise to the cause of the action,
  (i) a public authority or public corporation; or
  (ii) insured or otherwise indemnified in respect of the claim.

(2) In any case to which this section applies, the court may, on the application of the injured person, order—

(a) that the damages referred to in subsection (4)(a) below be awarded to the injured person; and

(b) that the injured person may apply for the further award of damages referred to in subsection (4)(b) below,

and the court may, if it considers it appropriate, order that an application under paragraph (b) above may be made only within a specified period.

(3) Where an injured person in respect of whom an award has been made under subsection (2)(a) above applies to the court for an award under subsection (2)(b) above, the court may award to the injured person the further damages referred to in subsection (4)(b) below.

(4) The damages referred to in subsections (2) and (3) above are—

(a) damages assessed on the assumption that the injured person will not develop the disease or suffer the deterioration in his condition; and

(b) further damages if he develops the disease or suffers the deterioration.

(5) Nothing in this section shall be construed—

(a) as affecting the exercise of any power relating to expenses including a power to make rules of court relating to expenses; or

(b) as prejudicing any duty of the court under any enactment or rule of law to reduce or limit the total damages which would have been recoverable apart from any such duty.

(6) The Secretary of State may, by order, provide that categories of defenders shall, for the purposes of paragraph (b) of subsection (1) above, become or cease to be responsible persons, and may make such modifications of that paragraph as appear to him to be necessary for the purpose.

And an order under this subsection shall be made by statutory instrument subject to annulment in pursuance of a resolution of either House of Parliament.

GENERAL NOTE

The section, which awards provisional damages for personal injuries, corresponds to s.6 of Pt. I and was originally framed in similar terms. It covers the situation where there is a risk that in the future, the injured person will, as a result of the act or omission giving rise to the action, develop some serious disease or suffer some serious deterioration in his physical or mental condition—subs. (1)(a).

In the words of the Lord Advocate, the principal change made at the report stage in the House of Lords "can be characterised as putting on the face of the primary legislation what had been intended to be left for rules of court" (see *Hansard,* H.L. (May 6, 1982), col. 1305).

It is specified in subs. (1)(b) that the responsible person must be a public authority or public corporation or, alternatively, insured or otherwise indemnified in respect of the claim. Moreover, it is specifically stated in subs. (2) that a court order for provisional damages be made "on the application of the injured person" so that, in the words of the Lord Advocate, "it is entirely up to the pursuer whether he goes for a final settlement of his claim or chooses to apply for provisional damages in the first instance with the possibility of a second instalment later" *ibid.* In the case of the latter, the court, where it considers it appropriate, may impose a time limit.

On the death of the injured person, the right to claim damages for the period to the date of death falls to his executor by virtue of s.2(1) of the Damages (Scotland) Act 1976.

Subs. (2) and (3) were redrafted to bring out the sequence of events and to clarify the point that the two amounts of damages referred to in subs. (4)(*a*) and (*b*) are not to be determined at the time of the original enquiry but that at this stage it is only the first award referred to in subs. (4)(*a*) which is quantified and an application made to postpone the balance which is to be assessed only when the court makes this second award under subs. (3).

Subs. (5): Unaltered at the report stage in the House of Lords, this states that (*a*) the court's power relating to expenses (including a power to make rules of court relating to these) remains unaffected while (*b*) the court's duty under any enactment or rule of law to reduce or limit the total damages which would have been recoverable remains unprejudiced.

Subs. (6): Introduced at the report stage in the House of Lords, this provides for the Secretary of State changing the categories of responsible persons by way of statutory instrument.

It was intended that the new provisions be given effect to, in any event, by rules of court, but the Lord President of the Court of Session considered it advisable that they be embodied in the Act itself (see *Hansard,* H.L. (May 6, 1982), col. 1305; the Lord Advocate). The section comes into operation when the Secretary of State by order appoints—s.76(3)(4).

Supplementary

13.—(1) In this Part of this Act, unless the context otherwise requires—

"personal injuries" includes any disease or any impairment of a person's physical or mental condition;

"relative", in relation to the injured person, means—

(*a*) the spouse or divorced spouse;

(*b*) any person, not being the spouse of the injured person, who was, at the time of the act or omission giving rise to liability in the responsible person, living with the injured person as husband or wife;

(*c*) any ascendant or descendant;

(*d*) any brother, sister, uncle or aunt; or any issue of any such person;

(*e*) any person accepted by the injured person as a child of his family.

In deducing any relationship for the purposes of the foregoing definition—

(*a*) any relationship by affinity shall be treated as a relationship by consanguinity; any relationship of the half blood shall be treated as a relationship of the whole blood; and the stepchild of any person shall be treated as his child; and

(*b*) an illegitimate person shall be treated as the legitimate child of his mother and reputed father.

(2) Any reference in this Part of this Act to a payment, benefit or pension shall be construed as a reference to any such payment, benefit or pension whether in cash or in kind.

(3) This Part of this Act binds the Crown.

General Note

Subs. (1): The subsection provides the interpretation of terms in use in Pt. II. It extends the term "personal injuries" to cover disease or mental or physical impairment, as well as defining the word "relative" which by amendment introduced at the report stage in the House of Commons now includes a cohabitee under (*b*) (see *Hansard,* H.C. (October 19, 1982), col. 294). The amendment, moved by the Solicitor-General for Scotland, is the result of the Government's recognition of an unmarried partner's right to damages in the light of the fact that "a significant minority of caring and stable relationships now exist outside marriage" (*ibid.*). A similar amendment, set out in s.3(1) of the present Act, having been moved by the Lord Chancellor at the report stage in the House of Lords (see *Hansard*, H.L. (May 4, 1982), col. 1105), was agreed to. This relates to the Fatal Accidents Act 1976 for England and Wales though the amendment in the present section reflects the wording to be found in s.18 of the Matrimonial Homes (Family Protection) (Scotland) Act 1981, which gives the cohabitee a limited right of occupancy. It should be noted, however, that unlike the position under s.1(3)(*b*)(ii) and (iii) of the Fatal Accidents Act, there is no precondition, before one is accepted as a cohabitee, of two years' residence in the same household as husband and wife. The provisions deliberately avoid elaboration, the issue being left for the courts to determine as a matter of fact (see *Hansard*, H.C. (October 19, 1982), col. 296: the Solicitor-General for Scotland). He added that it was for the courts to determine the appropriate level of the award (col. 297). It would, therefore, appear that a cohabitee will not necessarily be treated on all fours with a spouse. The subsection states that an illegitimate child shall be treated as the legitimate child of his mother and reputed father (see (*b*)).

Subs. (2): The subsection makes it clear that a payment, benefit or pension referred to in Pt. II can be in cash or in kind.

Subs. (3): The subsection states that Pt. II is binding on the Crown.

Amendment and repeal of enactments

14.—(1) Section 1(7) of the Damages (Scotland) Act 1976 is amended by inserting after the word "section" the words "or in Part II of the Administration of Justice Act 1982".

(2) Section 5 of that Act (provisions for the avoidance of multiplicity of actions) is repealed, and—

    (*a*) in section 4 of that Act the words "but this section is without prejudice to section 5 of this Act" shall cease to have effect, and

    (*b*) in section 6 of that Act—

        (i) in subsection (1) for the words "section 5 of this Act" there shall be substituted the words "this section", and

        (ii) after subsection (3) there shall be inserted—

            "(3) This section applies to any action in which, following the death of any person from personal injuries, damages are claimed—

            (*a*) by the executor of the deceased, in respect of the injuries from which the deceased died;

            (*b*) in respect of the death of the deceased, by any relative of his.".

(3) Notwithstanding section 73(5) of this Act, where an action to which section 5 of that Act applies has been raised and has not, prior to the commencement of subsection (2) above, been disposed of, the court shall not dismiss the action on the ground only that the pursuer has failed to serve notice of the action as required by subsection (6) of the said section 5.

(4) In section 10(2) of the said Act of 1976 (meaning of "deceased person's immediate family"), after the word "(*a*)" there shall be inserted the word "(*aa*)", and in paragraph 1 of Schedule 1 to that Act there shall be inserted after sub-paragraph (*a*) the following—

    "(*aa*) any person, not being the spouse of the deceased, who was, immediately before the deceased's death, living with the deceased as husband or wife;".

GENERAL NOTE

Subs. (2): the subsection repeals s.5 of the 1976 Act, a repeal recommended by the Scottish Law Commission (Scot. Law Com. No. 64 (1981) para. 16). The purpose of the repealed section was to avoid a multiplicity of actions but the means laid down proved cumbersome. In most instances, no difficulty is found in discovering the range of genuine claimants but s.5 imposed exacting requirements in the matter of tracing relatives and then serving notice of the action. The Scottish Law Commission further recommended that the most satisfactory solution would be for all the procedural requirements designed to avoid a multiplicity of actions to be contained in rules of court, any problems arising in practice being thereby swiftly remedied. The same subsection also contains consequential amendments following the repeal of s.5. It comes into operation when the Secretary of State by order so appoints—s.76(3)(4).

Subs. (3): The subsection was inserted at the report stage in the House of Lords and described by the Lord Advocate as a technical amendment to ensure that actions which have been raised can benefit from the repeal of s.5 immediately s.14(2) comes into force. In such actions, the burden of notifying all the relatives imposed by s.5 need not, in his words, "be pursued to the bitter end" (see *Hansard,* H.L. (May 6, 1982), col. 1305).

Subs. (4): In the interests of consistency, the same extension in respect of cohabitees appearing in s.13(1) is applied to the Damages (Scotland) Act 1976 (see *Hansard,* H.C. (October 19, 1982), col. 294: the Solicitor-General for Scotland). This is in respect of damages for both loss of support, which may be claimed by relatives of the deceased, and loss of society, restricted to claims from the immediate family.

PART III

POWERS OF COURTS TO AWARD INTEREST

Interest on debts and damages

15.—(1) The section set out in Part I of Schedule 1 to this Act shall be inserted after section 35 of the Supreme Court Act 1981.

(2) The section set out in Part II of that Schedule shall be inserted after section 97 of the County Courts Act 1959.

(3) The Crown Proceedings Act 1947 shall accordingly have effect subject to the amendment in Part III of that Schedule, being an amendment consequential on subsections (1) and (2) above.

(4) The provisions mentioned in subsection (5) below (which this section supersedes so far as they apply to the High Court and county courts) shall cease to have effect in relation to those courts.

(5) The provisions are—

    (*a*) section 3 of the Law Reform (Miscellaneous Provisions) Act 1934; and

    (*b*) in the Administration of Justice Act 1969—

        (i) section 22; and

        (ii) in section 34(3) the words from "and section 22" onwards.

(6) The section set out in Part IV of Schedule 1 to this Act shall be inserted after section 19 of the Arbitration Act 1950.

GENERAL NOTE

This section (which will come into operation on the making of an order by the Lord Chancellor—s.76(1),(2)) introduces new provisions as to the award by the High Court and county courts of interest on debts and damages, by way of a new s.35A of the Supreme Court Act 1981 and a new s.97A of the County Courts Act 1959, both of which are set out in Sched. 1 to this Act. The General Note to that Schedule should be consulted for the effect of the new provisions.

Subs. (1)–(3): See the general note to Sched. 1 to this Act.

Subs. (4) and (5): These provide that s.3 of the Law Reform (Miscellaneous Provisions) Act 1934, as amended by ss.22, 34(3) of the Administration of Justice Act 1969 shall no longer apply to the High Court and county courts. The provisions of s.3 of the 1934 Act (as amended by the 1969 Act) confer a discretion on all courts of record to award interest on debts and damages, which discretion must be exercised in the plaintiff's favour where damages for personal injuries are awarded (1969 Act, s.22). The award of interest can only be however, on the actual sum for which judgment is given and not on sums paid before judgment, whereas the new provisions introduced by s.15 and Sched. 1 of the present Act enable a judgment to award interest on all sums due to the plaintiff in respect of the cause of action, even though the whole or part of them have been paid by the defendant to the plaintiff *before judgment.* See further the general note to Sched. 1, below.

Subs. (6): See the general note to Sched. 1, Pt. IV to this Act.

Interest on lump sums in matrimonial proceedings

16. The following subsection shall be added after section 23(5) of the Matrimonial Causes Act 1973 (financial provision in orders in connection with divorce proceedings, etc.)—

"(6) Where the court—

    (*a*) makes an order under this section for the payment of a lump sum; and

    (*b*) directs—

        (i) that payment of that sum or any part of it shall be deferred; or

        (ii) that that sum or any part of it shall be paid by instalments.

the court may order that the amount deferred or the instalments shall carry interest at such rate as may be specified by the order from such date, not earlier than the date of the order, as may be so specified, until the date when payment of it is due.".

GENERAL NOTE

This section (which will come into operation on the making of an order by the Lord Chancellor—s.76(1), (2)) effects an amendment to s.23 of the Matrimonial Causes Act 1973 which is analogous to the power of the High Court or the county court to award interest on a judgment debt (see s.15 of and Sched. 1 to this Act). A new subs. (6) is added to s.23 of the 1973 Act to enable the court making an order under s.23 (*i.e.* on granting a decree of divorce, of nullity of marriage, or of judicial separation or at any time thereafter—s.23(1)) to order the payment of interest on any deferred payment of lump sum maintenance, but from no earlier date than the date of the order (*cf.* s.15 of and Sched. 1 to this Act).

PART IV

WILLS

Amendments of Wills Act 1837

Relaxation of formal requirements for making wills

17. The following section shall be substituted for section 9 of the Wills Act 1837—

"Signing and attestation of wills

9. No will shall be valid unless—

    (*a*) it is in writing, and signed by the testator, or by some other person in his presence and by his direction; and

    (*b*) it appears that the testator intended by his signature to give effect to the will; and

    (*c*) the signature is made or acknowledged by the testator in the presence of two or more witnesses present at the same time; and

    (*d*) each witness either—

        (i) attests and signs the will; or

        (ii) acknowledges his signature,

    in the presence of the testator (but not necessarily in the presence of any other witness),

but no form of attestation shall be necessary."

GENERAL NOTE

This section inserts a new s.9 into the Wills Act 1837, concerned with the formal requirements for making wills in England and Wales (for "international wills", see ss.27–28 below.) The new s.9 implements the recommendations of the Law Reform Committee's Report on the Making and Revocation of Wills (22nd Report, 1980, Cmnd. 7902, paras. 2.1 to 2.13). The new section relaxes the formal requirements for making wills in the ways indicated in the notes below to the new s.9. The rules as to valid informal wills (including oral wills) made by soldiers, sailors, etc., contained in s.11 of the Wills Act 1837 and the Wills (Soldiers and Sailors) Act 1918 remain in force and unchanged. This section comes into operation on January 1, 1983 and also does not apply to the will of a testator who dies before that date (ss.73(6), 76(11)).

S.9(a)

The requirement of signature by or on behalf of the testator was in the original s.9 of the Wills Act 1837 but the additional requirement of that section that the signature should be "at the foot or end" of the will is not repeated in the new section 9. The result is that the signature can be anywhere on the will *provided* (new s.9(*b*)) that "it appears that the testator intended by his signature to give effect to the will". The detailed interpretation of "foot or end" by s.1 of the Wills Act Amendment Act 1852 is consequently repealed, together with the rest of that Act, by s.72 of and Sched. 9, Pt. I, to this Act.

S.9(b)

This requirement is new. For its purpose, see the note to new s.9(*a*) above.

S.9(c)

This subsection merely repeats the identical provision of the original s.9 of the Wills Act 1837. When the testator signs (or acknowledges his signature), both witnesses must then be simultaneously present. They can then sign (or acknowledge their signatures) separately if they wish, provided they do it in the presence of the testator (see s.9(*d*) below).

S.9(d)

The requirement of the original s.9 of the Wills Act 1837 was that after the testator had signed (or acknowledged his signature) each witness should, in the presence of the testator, *sign* the will. This requirement is relaxed to allow a witness either to sign or to *acknowledge* his signature, thus validating a will made in circumstances such as those in *Re Colling* [1972] 1 W.L.R. 1440. The existing law that the witnesses need not sign (or, now, acknowledge) in the presence of each other is expressly stated.

"*but no form of attestation shall be necessary*": this phrase also occurred in the original s.9 of the Wills Act 1837.

Effect of marriage or its termination on wills

18.—(1) The following section shall be substituted for section 18 of the Wills Act 1837—

"Wills to be revoked by marriage, except in certain cases

18.—(1) Subject to subsections (2) to (4) below, a will shall be revoked by the testator's marriage.

(2) A disposition in a will in exercise of a power of appointment shall take effect notwithstanding the testator's subsequent marriage unless the property so appointed would in default of appointment pass to his personal representatives.

(3) Where it appears from a will that at the time it was made the testator was expecting to be married to a particular person and that he intended that the will should not be revoked by the marriage, the will shall not be revoked by his marriage to that person.

(4) Where it appears from a will that at the time it was made the testator was expecting to be married to a particular person and that he intended that a disposition in the will should not be revoked by his marriage to that person,—

(*a*) that disposition shall take effect notwithstanding the marriage; and

(*b*) any other disposition in the will shall take effect also, unless it appears from the will that the testator intended the disposition to be revoked by the marriage.".

(2) The following section shall be inserted after that section—

"Effect of dissolution or annulment of marriage on wills

18A.—(1) Where, after a testator has made a will, a decree of a court dissolves or annuls his marriage or declares it void,—

(*a*) the will shall take effect as if any appointment of the former spouse as an executor or as the executor and trustee of the will were omitted; and

(*b*) any devise or bequest to the former spouse shall lapse, except in so far as a contrary intention appears by the will.

(2) Subsection (1)(*b*) above is without prejudice to any right of the former spouse to apply for financial provision under the Inheritance (Provision for Family and Dependants) Act 1975.

(3) Where—

(*a*) by the terms of a will an interest in remainder is subject to a life interest; and

(*b*) the life interest lapses by virtue of subsection (1)(*b*) above,

the interest in remainder shall be treated as if it had not been subject to the life interest and, if it was contingent upon the termination of the life interest, as if it had not been so contingent.".

GENERAL NOTE

This section (by subs. (1)) implements the recommendations of the Law Reform Committee (1980, Cmnd. 7902), paras. 3.10; 3.11; and 3.18, that the exception to the rule that marriage revokes a will (certain exercises of powers of appointment and wills made in contemplation of marriage) should be brought up to date and rationalised. It also (by subs. (2)) makes limited provision for the effect of divorce or annulment of a marriage on the will of the former spouse, a matter on which the Law Reform Committee were unable to agree (see their Report, paras. 3.26–3.38). The section operates by substitution of new ss.18, 18A of the Wills Act 1837, with a consequent repeal (by s.75 and Sched. 9) of s.177 of the Law of Property Act 1925, dealing with wills in contemplation of marriage. This section comes into operation on January 1, 1983 (s.76(11)) *but* (*i*) s.18(1) (relating to the revocation of wills by marriage) and s.75 (and Sched. 9) (repealing s.177 of the Law of Property Act 1925 (c.20)), do not affect wills made before January 1, 1983 (s.73(7)); (*ii*) s.18(2), relating to the effect on a will of divorce or annulment, does not apply to the will of a testator dying before January 1, 1983 (s.73(*b*)).

Subs. (1): This subsection introduces a new s.18 of the Wills Act 1837, to take the place of the original s.18 and of s.177 of the Law of Property Act 1925 (see the General Note to s.18—above). The effect is annotated in the notes to the new s.18 of the 1837 Act (below).

S.18(1)

The rule that marriage of the testator revokes his or her will stems from the original s.18 of the Wills Act 1837, but is now made subject to the exceptions in subss. (2)–(4).

S.18(2)

This subsection substantially repeats the exception to the rule that the testator's marriage revokes a will, contained in the original s.18 of the Wills Act 1837 but brings it up to date by deleting obsolete references in the original s.18 to the testator's heir and the statute of distributions (see *Re Gilligan* [1950] P. 32). The exercise by will of a power of appointment is not revoked by the testator's marriage, unless the property would pass in default of appointment (*i.e.,* if the exercise were revoked) to the testator's personal representatives, *i.e.* as part of his estate, available for the new family created by his marriage.

Ss.18(3), (4)

The original exception, in s.177 of the Law of Property Act 1925, simply provided that "a will made in contemplation of a marriage" should not be revoked by that marriage. The language of the exception caused difficulties. In *Re Coleman* [1976] Ch. 1, for example, it was held that the whole will must be expressed to be made in contemplation of marriage (extrinsic evidence on the point not being admissible) and that such contemplation could not be deduced from certain gifts to a named fiancé(e). Now, ss.20 and 21 of this Act relax to a certain extent the rules as to the admissibility of extrinsic evidence of a testator's intentions and ss.(3), (4) of the new s.18 of the Wills Act 1837 deal with the kind of difficulties experienced in *Re Coleman* (*supra*). In effect the subsections give effect to the recommendations of the Law Reform Committee (para. 3.18) that s.177 of the Law of Property Act 1925 "should be amended to make it clear that, if a will *or any part* of a will is shown by its language to be intended to survive a particular marriage, the presumption should be that the whole will was intended to survive, such presumption to be rebuttable in respect of any one or more bequests revealing a contrary intention."

Subs.(2):
S.18A

This section is new and resolves the disagreement among the members of the Law Reform Committee (Report, paras. 3.26–3.38). Under the Wills Act 1837, divorce or annulment had no effect on the will(s) of the parties to the marriage. However, under this section the ending of the marriage in any way by decree of the court (divorce, annulment, or recognition that a marriage was voidable) has the following effects on the will(s) of the former spouses, except so far as a contrary intention appears in the will:

(i)   any appointment of a former spouse as an executor or executor/trustee is ineffective and a grant of letters of administration with the will annexed may be necessary (subs. (1)).

(ii) any devise or bequest to the former spouse will lapse and the relevant property will fall into residue or (if no residue) pass on intestacy (subs. (1)), unless it is a life interest, as to which see (iii) below;

(iii) any interest in remainder (vested or contingent) dependent on the termination of a spouse's life interest will be accelerated by the lapse of the life interest under (ii) above (subs. (3));

The former spouse, affected by (ii) or (iii) above, may still make a claim for "reasonable financial provision" under the Inheritance (Provision for Family and Dependants) Act 1975 (subs. (2)).

Gifts to children, etc. who predecease testator

19. The following section shall be substituted for section 33 of the Wills Act 1837—

> **"Gifts to children or other issue who leave issue living at the testator's death shall not lapse**
>
> **33.**—(1) Where—
>   (*a*) a will contains a devise or bequest to a child or remoter descendant of the testator; and
>   (*b*) the intended beneficiary dies before the testator, leaving issue; and
>   (*c*) issue of the intended beneficiary are living at the testator's death,
> then, unless a contrary intention appears by the will, the devise or bequest shall take effect as a devise or bequest to the issue living at the testator's death.
>
> (2) Where—
>   (*a*) a will contains a devise or bequest to a class of persons consisting of children or remoter descendants of the testator; and
>   (*b*) a member of the class dies before the testator, leaving issue; and
>   (*c*) issue of that member are living at the testator's death,
> then, unless a contrary intention appears by the will, the devise or bequest shall take effect as if the class included the issue of its deceased member living at the testator's death.
>
> (3) Issue shall take under this section through all degrees, according to their stock, in equal shares if more than one, any gift or share which their parent would have taken and so that no issue shall take whose parent is living at the testator's death and so capable of taking.
>
> (4) For the purposes of this section—
>   (*a*) the illegitimacy of any person is to be disregarded; and
>   (*b*) a person conceived before the testator's death and born

living thereafter is to be taken to have been living at the testator's death.".

GENERAL NOTE

This section comes into operation on January 1, 1983 (s.76(11)) but does not affect the will of a testator who dies before that date (s.73(6)). It provides a substituted section 33 in the Wills Act 1837, intended to remove the anomalies caused by the original s.33. Both the original and the new section 33 constitute exceptions from the rule that a devise or bequest lapses if the donee predeceases the testator. The exception is in favour of children or remoter issue who predecease the testator, leaving their issue who are alive at the testator's death. The original s.33 preserved the gift in such circumstances but merely transferred it to the estate of the deceased child, etc., with the result that it might not pass to that child's issue but could go under a gift elsewhere of residue in that child's will, or pass to his creditors or trustee in bankruptcy. Consequently the new s.33 makes in effect a direct transfer of such a devise or legacy to the issue of the deceased (child, etc.) legatee (new s.33(1)). If it were a class gift, the deceased donee's share passes *per stirpes* (according to the stock) to that donee's issue (new s.33(3)). The "direct transfer" is subject to a contrary intention, *i.e.* an intention that the normal rule of lapse shall operate. As to evidence of contrary intention, see *Re Morris* (1916), 86 L.J.Ch. 456; *Re Wilson* (1920), 89 L.J.Ch. 216 and *Re Meredith* [1924] 2 Ch. 552. This evidence must be collected from the words of the will itself and cannot be ascertained by extrinsic evidence (see the notes to ss.20, 21, below).

S.33(1)–(3)

See the General Note above for the effect of these subsections. "Issue" includes descendants to any remote degree, including illegitimate relationships (s.33(4)(*a*)).

S.33(4)

(*a*) The extension to illegitimate relationships follows the provision to this effect of s.16 of the Family Law Reform Act 1969, now repealed by s.75 of and Sched. 9, Pt. I, to the present Act.

(*b*) Issue *en ventre sa mère* at the date of the testator's death is deemed to have been alive at that death, so as to bring the provisions of the new section 33 into operation.

Rectification and interpretation of wills

Rectification

20.—(1) If a court is satisfied that a will is so expressed that it fails to carry out the testator's intentions, in consequence—

(*a*) of a clerical error; or

(*b*) of a failure to understand his instructions,

it may order that the will shall be rectified so as to carry out his intentions.

(2) An application for an order under this section shall not, except with the permission of the court, be made after the end of the period of six months from the date on which representation with respect to the estate of the deceased is first taken out.

(3) The provisions of this section shall not render the personal representatives of a deceased person liable for having distributed any part of the estate of the deceased, after the end of the period of six months from the date on which representation with respect to the estate of the deceased is first taken out, on the ground that they ought to have taken into account the possibility that the court might permit the making of an application for an order under this section after the end of that period; but this subsection shall not prejudice any power to recover, by reason of the making of an order under this section, any part of the estate so distributed.

(4) In considering for the purposes of this section when representation with respect to the estate of a deceased person was first taken out, a grant limited to settled land or to trust property shall be left out of account, and a grant limited to real estate or to personal estate shall be left out of account unless a grant limited to the remainder of the estate has previously been made or is made at the same time.

GENERAL NOTE

This section amends the law, in accordance with the recommendations of the Law Reform Committee on the Interpretation of Wills (1973, Cmnd. 5301). It comes into operation on

January 1, 1983 (s.76(11)) but does not affect the wills of testators who died before that date (s.73(6)). Under this section, the court can (subject to rigid limits—see below) admit evidence, which *ex hypothesi* must be extrinsic (*cf.*, s.21 below), to show that a will is so expressed that it fails to carry out the testator's intentions and, if satisfied that that is so, the court can order the rectification of the will so as to carry out the testator's intentions. However, the evidence is admissible only to show that the failure to carry out the testator's intentions is due to a clerical error or to failure to understand the testator's instructions. Extrinsic evidence is not admissible generally to show that a will does not accord with a testator's intentions (*cf.*, s.21(1)(c) below). For circumstances where rectification may now be sought, see *Re Reynette-James* [1976] 1 W.L.R. 161.

Subs. (1): A rectification order will presumably be analogous to an order to rectify a contract and will be made in exercise of Chancery jurisdiction. For the circumstances in which such an order can be made, see the General Note above.

Subs. (2), (4): Except with the permission of the court, application for a rectification order cannot be made after the end of six months from the date on which a grant of probate or of letters of administration (with the will annexed) is first taken out (subs. (2)). Time does not run from the taking out of a grant limited to settled land or trust property, or to a grant limited to realty or to personalty unless there is a co-existent grant to the remainder of the estate (subs. (4)).

Subs. (3): This subsection exonerates personal representatives from any personal liability for having distributed any part of the estate after six months from the first grant of representation (as to which see above), according to the literal words of the will, "on the ground that they ought to have taken into account the possibility that the court might permit the making of an application" after the six months for a rectification order under this section. If the court has already given its permission, presumably the personal representatives would distribute at their peril. The exoneration of the personal representatives does not in any event prevent those entitled under the will as rectified from tracing the assets into the hands of those who have received them and attempting to recover them (for the circumstances in which this can be done, see *Ministry of Health* v. *Simpson* [1951] A.C. 251).

Interpretation of wills—general rules as to evidence

21.—(1) This section applies to a will—
   (*a*) in so far as any part of it is meaningless;
   (*b*) in so far as the language used in any part of it is ambiguous on the face of it;
   (*c*) in so far as evidence, other than evidence of the testator's intention, shows that the language used in any part of it is ambiguous in the light of surrounding circumstances.

(2) In so far as this section applies to a will extrinsic evidence, including evidence of the testator's intention, may be admitted to assist in its interpretation.

GENERAL NOTE
   This section comes into force on January 1, 1983 (s.76(11)) and does not apply to the will of a testator dying before that date (s.73(6)). It implements recommendations of the Law Reform Committee on Interpretation of Wills (1973, Cmnd. 5301). It replaces the complex case law on the subject by restating the principles including the admissibility of extrinsic evidence to construe a testator's will. The principle is that only the words of a testator in a properly made will (as to which, see s.17 above) are to have testamentary effect and evidence of the testator's intention is not admissible to *contradict* the words of the will, save where rectification is possible under s.20 above. If, however, the words of the will are meaningless or in themselves ambiguous, either on the face of the will (patent ambiguity) or because extrinsic evidence (*not* at this stage to include evidence of the testator's intention) shows them to be so (latent ambiguity) then extrinsic evidence, including evidence of the testator's intention, may be admitted "to assist in" the resolution of the meaninglessness or the ambiguity. If the extrinsic evidence fails to resolve the matter, the gift may be held to be void for uncertainty—*Richardson* v. *Watson* (1833) 4 B. & Ad. 787.

Presumption as to effect of gifts to spouses

22. Except where a contrary intention is shown it shall be presumed that if a testator devises or bequeaths property to his spouse in terms which in themselves would give an absolute interest to the spouse, but by the same instrument purports to give his issue an interest in the same property, the gift to the spouse is absolute notwithstanding the purported gift to the issue.

GENERAL NOTE

This section comes into force on January 1, 1983 (s.76(11)) and does not apply to the will of a testator dying before that date (s.73(6)). It implements a recommendation of the Law Reform Committee on the Interpretation of Wills (1973, Cmnd. 5301). This section applies to the type of gift often found in a home-made will, whereby the testator gives, for example, "All my property to my wife and after her death to our children." This would normally be held to confer only a life interest on the wife, despite the apparent absolute gift to her in the first instance, because of the need to preserve the apparent remainder to the children. This is probably contrary to the intention of the testator who intends to give the property absolutely to his wife but to have a say over its ultimate destination. Consequently, this section provides that unless a contrary intention is shown (which must be collected from the words of the will itself and cannot be ascertained by extrinsic evidence—see the General Notes to ss.20, 21 above), the gift to the spouse is absolute and the purported gift to the issue fails. This is so, even if the gifts to the spouse and the issue are in separate parts of the will. The section applies only to gifts to a spouse and issue (including grandchildren, etc.) and does not apply to gifts to others, for example a cohabitee or nephews and nieces. For the position where the marriage has terminated by divorce, etc., see s.18(2) above.

Registration of wills

Deposit and registration of wills of living persons

23.—(1) The following, namely—

   (*a*) the Principal Registry of the Family Division of the High Court of Justice;

   (*b*) the Keeper of the Registers of Scotland; and

   (*c*) the Probate and Matrimonial Office of the Supreme Court of Northern Ireland,

shall be registering authorities for the purposes of this section.

(2) Each registering authority shall provide and maintain safe and convenient depositories for the custody of the wills of living persons.

(3) Any person may deposit his will in such a depository in accordance with regulations under section 25 below and on payment of the prescribed fee.

(4) It shall be the duty of a registering authority to register in accordance with regulations under section 25 below—

   (*a*) any will deposited in a depository maintained by the authority; and

   (*b*) any other will whose registration is requested under Article 6 of the Registration Convention.

(5) A will deposited in a depository provided—

   (*a*) under section 172 of the Supreme Court of Judicature (Consolidation) Act 1925 or section 126 of the Supreme Court Act 1981; or

   (*b*) under Article 27 of the Administration of Estates (Northern Ireland) Order 1979,

shall be treated for the purposes of this section as if it had been deposited under this section.

(6) In this section "prescribed" means—

   (*a*) in the application of this section to England and Wales, prescribed by an order under section 130 of the Supreme Court Act 1981;

   (*b*) in its application to Scotland, prescribed by an order under section 26 below; and

   (*c*) in its application to Northern Ireland, prescribed by an order under section 116 of the Judicature (Northern Ireland) Act 1978.

This section comes into operation on such date as the Lord Chancellor and the Secretary of State may by order jointly appoint (s.76(5)). It will enable the United Kingdom to ratify the Council of Europe Convention on the Registration of Wills (Basle, May 16, 1972). The section provides for facilities for the deposit and registration in England and Wales, Scotland, and Northern Ireland of the wills of living persons including "international wills" (see ss.27–28 below). The registration will facilitate the giving and receiving of information as to deposited wills (see s.24 below). There is no provision that the registration of a will guarantees its validity, though regulations to be made under s.25 (below) may presumably contain requirements designed to ensure the *prima facie* validity of a will.

Subs. (2): Depositories for the wills of living persons already exist in London and in Belfast under the aegis of the Principal Registry of the Family Division of the High Court (see subs. (5) below) and of the Probate and Matrimonial Office of the Supreme Court of Northern Ireland. These will continue to have effect under this section (see subs. (5) below), but this section also provides for registration in accordance with the 1972 Convention and for the establishment of a depository in Scotland.

Subs. (3): There is no limitation in this subsection or in s.25 below on the nationality, etc., of a person depositing a will, though only the testator himself can do so.

Subs. (4)(b): Art. 6 of the Convention enables registries in other countries to request registration of a will in a depository in the United Kingdom and *vice versa*—see s.24(1)(*a*) below.

Subs. (5): See the note to subs. (2) above. These statutory provisions provide only for the deposit (not registration) of wills. S.172 of the 1925 Act was repealed, together with the rest of that Act by s.152(4) of and Sched. 7 to the Supreme Court Act 1981.

Subs. 6: See the note to s.26 (below).

Designation of Principal Registry as national body under Registration Convention

24.—(1) The Principal Registry of the Family Division of the High Court of Justice shall be the national body for the purposes of the Registration Convention, and shall accordingly have the functions assigned to the national body by the Registration Convention including, without prejudice to the general application of the Convention to the Principal Registry by virtue of this section, the function—

(*a*) of arranging for the registration of wills in other Contracting States as provided for in Article 6 of the Convention;

(*b*) of receiving and answering requests for information arising from the national bodies of other Contracting States.

(2) In this Part of this Act "the Registration Convention" means the Convention on the Establishment of a Scheme of Registration of Wills concluded at Basle on 16th May 1972.

This section (which comes into operation on such date as the Lord Chancellor and the Secretary of State may by order jointly appoint—s.76(5)) makes the Principal Registry in London of the Family Division of the High Court of Justice the "national" body for the whole of the United Kingdom for fulfilling the functions (see subs. (1)(*a*), (*b*)) assigned to the national body by the 1972 Convention (see subs. (2)).

Regulations as to deposit and registration of wills, etc.

25.—(1) Regulations may make provision—

(*a*) as to the conditions for the deposit of a will;

(*b*) as to the manner of and procedure for—

　　(i) the deposit and registration of a will; and

　　(ii) the withdrawal of a will which has been deposited; and

　　(iii) the cancellation of the registration of a will; and

(*c*) as to the manner in which the Principal Registry of the Family Division is to perform its functions as the national body under the Registration Convention.

(2) Regulations under this section may contain such incidental or supplementary provisions as the authority making the regulations considers appropriate.

(3) Any such regulations are to be made—

  (a) for England and Wales, by the President of the Family Division of the High Court of Justice, with the concurrence of the Lord Chancellor;

  (b) for Scotland, by the Secretary of State after consultation with the Lord President of the Court of Session; and

  (c) for Northern Ireland, by the Northern Ireland Supreme Court Rules Committee, with the concurrence of the Lord Chancellor.

(4) Regulations made by virtue of subsection (1)(c) above shall be made by the Lord Chancellor.

(5) Subject to subsection (6) below, regulations under this section shall be made by statutory instrument and shall be laid before Parliament after being made.

(6) Regulations for Northern Ireland shall be statutory rules for the purposes of the Statutory Rules (Northern Ireland) Order 1979; and any such statutory rule shall be laid before Parliament after being made in like manner as a statutory instrument and section 4 of the Statutory Instruments Act 1946 shall apply accordingly.

(7) The Statutory Instruments Act 1946 shall apply to a statutory instrument containing regulations made in accordance with subsection (3)(a) or (c) above as if the regulations had been made by a Minister of the Crown.

(8) Any regulations made under section 172 of the Supreme Court of Judicature (Consolidation) Act 1925 or section 126 of the Supreme Court Act 1981 shall have effect for the purposes of this Part of this Act as they have effect for the purposes of the enactment under which they were made.

GENERAL NOTE

This section comes into operation on such date as the Lord Chancellor and the Secretary of State may by order jointly appoint (s.76(5)). It empowers the making of regulations for the purposes set out in subs. (1). The procedure for making the regulations will be that applicable to statutory instruments by the Statutory Instruments Act 1946. Regulations (for example, as to fees for deposit) under the existing statutory provisions for depositories continue to have effect for the purposes of this Part of the Act (s.25(8) and *cf.*, s.23(5) above).

Fees as to registration in Scotland

26. The Secretary of State may, with the consent of the Treasury, from time to time by order made by statutory instrument fix fees payable in respect of—

  (a) the deposit, registration or withdrawal of wills under this Act;

  (b) the obtaining of information from the register; and

  (c) any other thing which the Keeper of the Registers of Scotland is required or authorised to do under this Act or any regulations made thereunder in connection with the depositing or registration of wills.

GENERAL NOTE

This section applies only to Scotland and comes into operation on January 1, 1983 (s.76(11)). Fees payable in England and Wales and in Northern Ireland are governed by orders made under the existing legislation for depositories (see ss.23(6) and 25(8) above).

International wills

The form of an international will

27.—(1) The Annex to the Convention on International Wills shall have the force of law in the United Kingdom.

(2) The Annex is set out in Schedule 2 to this Act.

(3) In this Part of this Act—

"international will" means a will made in accordance with the requirements of the Annex, as set out in Schedule 2 to this Act; and

"the Convention on International Wills" means the Convention providing a Uniform Law on the Form of an International Will concluded at Washington on 26th October, 1973.

GENERAL NOTE

This section and s.28 below concern "international wills" and will enable the United Kingdom to ratify the 1973 Convention on International Wills (the "Unidroit" Convention—see full title in s.27(3)). Both sections come into operation on such day as the Lord Chancellor and the Secretary of State may by order jointly appoint (s.76(5)), which will presumably not be until the United Kingdom ratifies the Convention. This section accords the force of law to the Annex to the 1973 Convention, which is set out in Sched. 2 and contains detailed requirements as to the *formal* validity of a will (as distinct from *essential* validity—for example, the capacity of a testator to make the will—normally governed by the law of the testator's domicile), for it to be recognised as valid by the countries which eventually sign and ratify the Convention. A will thus made is termed an "international will" and will also in fact be valid under United Kingdom domestic law (see the new section 9 of the Wills Act 1837, introduced by s.17 above). The revocation of such a will is governed by the appropriate domestic law (Sched. 2, art. 14), for example, in the United Kingdom s.20–21 of the Wills Act 1837 and s.18 of the present Act.

Comparison should be made with the Wills Act 1963 (c.44), which was the prelude to ratification by the United Kingdom of the Hague Convention on the Formal Validity of Wills (1961, Cmnd. 1729). S.1 of the 1963 Act provides that a will shall be treated as properly executed (*i.e.* formally valid) if its execution conformed to the internal law in force in the territory where it was executed, or in the territory where, at the time of its execution, or of the testator's death, he was domiciled or had his habitual residence, or in a state of which, at either of those times, he was a national. S.2 of the 1963 Act provides additional rules for formal validity of wills made on ships or aircraft, or disposing of land, revoking a prior will, or exercising a power of appointment. The 1963 Act is, of course, concerned with internal recognition by the United Kingdom of wills with a "foreign" element. S.27 and 28 of the present Act are concerned with "international" validity of a will.

International wills—procedure

28.—(1) The persons authorised to act in the United Kingdom in connection with international wills are—

(*a*) solicitors; and

(*b*) notaries public.

(2) A person who is authorised under section 6(1) of the Commissioners for Oaths Act 1889 to do notarial acts in any foreign country or place is authorised to act there in connection with international wills.

(3) An international will certified by virtue of subsection (1) or (2) above may be deposited in a depository provided under section 23 above.

(4) Section 23 above shall accordingly have effect in relation to such international wills.

(5) Subject to subsection (6) below, regulations under section 25 above shall have effect in relation to such international wills as they have effect in relation to wills deposited under section 23 above.

(6) Without prejudice to the generality of section 25 above, regulations under that section may make special provision with regard to such international wills.

(7) In section 10 of the Consular Relations Act 1968 (by virtue of which diplomatic agents and consular officials may administer oaths and do notarial acts in certain cases)—

(*a*) at the end of subsection (1)(*b*) there shall be added the words "or (*c*) in connection with an international will."; and

(*b*) at the end of subsection (4) there shall be added the words "and "international will" has the meaning assigned to it by section 27 of the Administration of Justice Act 1982".

GENERAL NOTE

See the General Note to s.27 above, concerning the nature of "international wills". This section comes into operation on such day as the Lord Chancellor and the Secretary of State may by order jointly appoint (s.76(5)). It defines for the various purposes of the Annex to the Convention (set out in Sched. 2 to this Act) "the authorised person" who has the important functions set out in that Annex (for example as to the drawing-up of the appropriate certificate—art. 10). Such authorised persons are solicitors (in England, Wales and Scotland); notaries public; and in certain circumstances British ambassadors, envoys, counsellors and diplomatic agents and consular officials, etc., of other states (subss. (1), (2), (7)). Certified international wills may be deposited in the registries provided for under s.23 above (subss. (3)–(6)).

Subs. (2): Such persons include British ambassadors, envoys, ministers, chargés d'affaires, consuls, and counsellors exercising their functions outside the United Kingdom—see also s.3 of the Oaths and Evidence (Overseas Authorities and Countries) Act 1963 (c.27).

Subs. (7): S.10 of the Consular Relations Act 1968 empowers diplomatic agents or consular officers of any State to administer oaths and do notarial acts if required by a person for use in that state or under the laws thereof or otherwise required by a national of that State but not for use in the United Kingdom except under the laws of some other country (s.10(1)). Such powers are now extended to those contained in the Annex to the 1973 Convention (set out in Sched. 2 to this Act) for "authorised persons".

PART V

COUNTY COURTS

County court districts

29.—(1) The Lord Chancellor may by order specify places at which county courts are to be held and the name by which the court held at any place so specified is to be known.

(2) Any order under this section shall be made by statutory instrument, which shall be laid before Parliament after being made.

(3) The district for which county courts are to be held shall be determined in accordance with directions given by or on behalf of the Lord Chancellor.

(4) Subject to any alterations made by virtue of this section, county courts shall continue to be held for the districts and at the places and by the names appointed at the commencement of this section.

GENERAL NOTE

This section comes into operation on January 1, 1983 (s.76(11)). The explanatory memorandum to the Bill described its purpose as to facilitate the definition of county court districts when new courts are added or old ones are closed.

Residence of registrars

30. Section 25 of the County Courts Act 1959 (which obliges a county court registrar to reside in the district for which he is registrar, except with the consent of the Lord Chancellor and subject to such conditions as the Lord Chancellor may impose) shall cease to have effect.

GENERAL NOTE

This section comes into operation on January 1, 1983 (s.76(11)). It provides that a county court registrar no longer needs the consent of the Lord Chancellor to reside outside his court district.

Arrest in Admiralty proceedings

31. The following subsections shall be substituted for subsections (9) and (10) of section 57 of the County Courts Act 1959 (which provides for the mode of exercise of the Admiralty jurisdiction of a county court)—

"(9) A county court may issue a warrant for the arrest and detention of any vessel, aircraft or property to which an action in rem brought in the court relates unless or until bail to the amount of the claim made in the action and the reasonable costs of the plaintiff in the action be entered into and perfected by or on behalf of the defendant.

(10) except as provided by subsection (9) of this section, no vessel, aircraft or property shall be arrested or detained in Admiralty proceedings in a county court otherwise than in execution.".

GENERAL NOTE

This section comes into operation on January 1, 1983 (s.76(11)). It substitutes new subss. (9), (10) in s.57 of the County Courts Act 1959, which section was itself substituted by s.149(1) of and Sched. 3 to the Supreme Court Act 1981. The former subss. (9), (10) made the county court's power to issue a warrant contingent on the court's being satisfied that it was probable that the vessel, aircraft, or property to which the proceedings related would be removed out of the jurisdiction. There is no such restriction in the new subss. (9) (10) and the county court will have under them substantially the same power of arrest as that exercised by the High Court.

Jurisdiction in relation to counterclaims, etc.

32. The following section shall be inserted after section 75C of the County Courts Act 1959—

"Jurisdiction to deal with counterclaim or set-off and counterclaim
75D. If the condition specified in section 75C(1) (*c*) of this Act is satisfied, but—
(*a*) no application is made for an order under that section; or
(*b*) an application for such an order is made but is refused,
the county court shall have jurisdiction to deal with the counterclaim or set-off and counterclaim.".

GENERAL NOTE

This section came into operation on the day that the Act was passed, namely October 28, 1982 (s.76(9) and (10)). The effect of the section is to allow the county court to adjudicate on a counter-claim or set-off, even if it exceeds a financial or other jurisdictional limit on the county court's jurisdiction (as to the financial or other jurisdictional limit, see the note to s.37 below). The reference to s.75C of the County Courts Act 1959 (c.22) is to that section as inserted by s.149(1) of and Sched. 3 to the Supreme Court Act 1981. S.75C concerns transfer of proceedings to the High Court by order of the county court where, *inter alia,* "any counterclaim or set-off and counterclaim of a defendant involves matters beyond the jurisdiction of the county court" (s.75C(1)). The present section operates only where there is no order for transfer to the High Court, either by the county court of its own motion or an application by a party.

County court rules

33.—(1) The following paragraph shall be inserted after section 102(3)(*b*) of the County Courts Act 1959—

"(*bb*) prescribing the circumstances in which a warrant for the arrest and detention of any vessel, aircraft or property to which an action in rem relates may be transferred from one court to another and the procedure consequent on any such transfer;".

(2) Without prejudice to the generality of subsection (1) of the said section 102, county court rules may regulate or provide for any matters which were regulated or provided for by county court rules which were made at any time before 1st January 1982.

GENERAL NOTE

This section comes into operation on January 1, 1983 (s.76(11)).

Subs. (1): This subsection is complementary to s.31 of this Act and the General Note to that section should be consulted.

Subs. (2): This subsection permits county court rules to make provision for any matter provided for by the county court rules in force before the amendments made by the County Court Amendment Rules, 1981 (S.I. 1981 Nos. 1661 and 1775) came into operation on January 1, 1982. See now the current County Court Rules 1981 (operative September 1, 1982), S.I. 1981 No. 1687.

Transfers from High Court to county court

34.—(1) The following section shall be substituted for section 139 of the County Courts Act 1959—

"Enforcement in county court of judgments and orders of High Court
139. A judgment or order of the High Court for the payment of money to a person, and any judgment, order, decree or award (however called) of any court or arbitrator (including any foreign court or foreign arbitrator) being a judgment, order, decree or award for the payment of money to a person which is or has become enforceable (whether wholly or to a limited extent) as if it were a judgment or order of the High Court shall be enforceable in the county court as if it were a judgment of that court.".

(2) In section 148 of that Act (administration orders)—
  (*a*) in subsection (1)—
      (i) the words "in a county court" shall cease to have effect; and
      (ii) for the words "that court" there shall be substituted the words "a county court"; and
  (*b*) subsection (2) shall cease to have effect.

(3) In section 1(2)(*c*) of the Charging Orders Act 1979 (by virtue of which certain High Court orders for an amount exceeding £5,000 must be enforced in the High Court) after the words "High Court" in the second place where they occur, there shall be inserted the words "or a county court".

GENERAL NOTE

This section comes into force on a day to be appointed by order of the Lord Chancellor (s.76(1), (2)). It is concerned with the enforcement by the county court of High Court judgments and orders.

Subs. (1): This subsection substantially reproduces the wording of the original s.139 of the County Courts Act 1959, but without the words "on an application's being made to the county court by the party prosecuting the judgment".

Subs. (2): This subsection amends s.148 of the County Courts Act 1959, which allows the county court to administer the "estate" of a debtor whose indebtedness he alleges does not exceed £5,000 (S.I. 1981 No. 1122), by allowing the county court to make the order where the debtor is unable to pay forthwith the judgment of any court (for example, the High Court). Previously, the power was restricted to cases of inability to pay county court judgments.

Subs. (3): The effect of this amendment of s.1(2)(*c*) of the Charging Orders Act 1979 is to enable the county court, as well as the High Court, to make a charging order in respect of a High Court judgment or order for an amount exceeding £5,000.

Transfers from county court to High Court

35. The following shall be inserted after section 139 of the County Courts Act 1959—

"Enforcement in High Court of judgments and orders of county courts

139A.—(1) If—

(*a*) a judgment or order for the payment of a sum of money has been given or made by a county court; and

(*b*) an amount in respect of that sum exceeding the amount for the time being specified for the purposes of this section by an order under subsection (3) of this section has become recoverable by execution,

the judgment or order may, subject to rules of court, be transferred to the High Court.

(2) A judgment or order transferred to the High Court by virtue of subsection (1) above may be enforced in the High Court as if it were a judgment or order of that court and shall be treated as a judgment or order of the High Court for all purposes except—

(*a*) that powers to set aside, correct, vary or quash a judgment or order of a county court shall continue to be exercisable in relation to it and powers to set aside, correct, vary or quash a judgment or order of the High Court shall not be exercisable; and

(*b*) that enactments relating to appeals from a judgment or order of a county court shall continue to apply to it and enactments relating to appeals from a judgment or order of the High Court shall not apply.

(3) The Lord Chancellor may by order specify an amount for the purposes of subsection (1) of this section; and any such order may specify different amounts for different descriptions of judgment or order.

(4) An order under subsection (3) of this section shall be made by statutory instrument and shall be subject to annulment in pursuance of a resolution of either House of Parliament.".

GENERAL NOTE

This section comes into operation on a day to be appointed by order of the Lord Chancellor (s.76(1), (2)). Introducing this clause in the Bill, the Lord Chancellor explained (*Hansard*, H.L. Vol. 428, col. 32) that in deference to professional and public opinion, under-sheriffs should be permitted to enforce a limited category of county court judgments, as an alternative to the county court bailiffs. He indicated that he proposed under the new s.139A(3) of the County Courts Act 1959 to fix by order a figure of £2,000 and over for judgments and orders of the county court to be eligible for enforcement in the High Court (corresponding to the increase in 1981 of the county court's jurisdiction from £2,000 to £5,000).

S.139A(1)

For the financial limit see subs. (3) and also the General Note to this section.

S.139A(2)

This subsection makes it clear that a transferred judgment or order of the county court is to be regarded as a High Court judgment or order in effect only for enforcement purposes and not for example for the setting-aside of or appeal from such a judgment or order.

S.139A(3)

For the proposed financial limit, see the General Note to this section.

Proceedings against mortgage guarantors

36. In section 38(1) of the Administration of Justice Act 1970 (county court jurisdiction to hear and determine certain actions for possession of mortgaged land notwithstanding that a claim for payment by the mortgagor of the amount owing in respect of the mortgage is also made in the action and that by reason of the amount claimed the last-mentioned claim is not within the jurisdiction of a county court) for the words "for payment by the mortgagor of the amount owing in respect of the mortgage is also made in the action" there shall be substituted the words "is also made in the action for payment by the mortgagor of the amount owing in respect of the mortgage or for payment of that amount by any person who guaranteed the debt secured by the mortgage".

GENERAL NOTE

This section came into operation on the day this Act was passed, namely October 28, 1982 (s.76(9), (10)). It amends s.38(1) of the Administration of Justice Act 1970, which allows a county court to entertain a mortgagee's claim for possession of mortgaged land even though the mortgagee also claims a sum due as the mortgage debt, exceeding the financial jurisdiction of the county court (now £5,000—see s.37 below). The amendment allows this to occur, even if the claim for the mortgage debt is not against the mortgagor (the only provision of the original s.38(1) of the 1970 Act) but is against a guarantor of the mortgage debt.

Limits of county court jurisdiction

37. The enactments specified in Schedule 3 to this Act shall have effect subject to the amendments specified in that Schedule, being amendments to restate the limits of county court jurisdiction and to provide for the raising of those limits.

GENERAL NOTE

This section comes into operation on January 1, 1983 (s.76(11)). Its purpose was defined by the explanatory memorandum to the Bill as to reorganise the many provisions regarding the monetary limits on the county court jurisdiction so as to provide an integrated scheme. This is done by collecting the statutory provisions together in Sched. 3 to this Act and inserting in them, in substitution for a specified financial limit, a reference simply to "the county court limit" being the general limit set by order under s.192 of the County Courts Act 1959, a new version of which (to fit the generality required of the Order) is substituted by Pt. III of Sched. 3. The present normal financial limit is £5,000, set by the County Courts Jurisdiction Order 1981 (S.I. 1981 No. 1123).

PART VI

FUNDS IN COURT

GENERAL NOTE

This Part of the Act was introduced by the Lord Chancellor as follows (*Hansard,* Vol. 428, cols. 32–33):

"Part VI . . . restates more concisely and in modern terms the main statute law controlling the management and investment of funds in court. It replaces the separate statutory provisions for funds in the High Court and the county courts now contained in Part I of the Administration of Justice Act 1965 and Part X of the County Courts Act 1959 with a single statutory framework for dealing with money held or paid into those courts. It also clears away the present detailed and restrictive legislation which the Accountant General has found in recent years to be too inflexible in conducting the investment of funds in court in modern economic conditions . . . while the essential framework of the legislation relating to the management of funds in court is retained, it is restated in the broadest terms and the administrative detail previously dealt with on the face of the statute will be contained in rules.

This Part of the Act comes into operation on a day or days to be appointed by order of the Lord Chancellor (ss.38–47) or by order of the Secretary of State (s.48)—s.76(1), (2), (3), (4). Until that time, certain transitional amendments are effected by s.73(8)—see the General Note to that subsection, below.

Definitions of various words and phrases used in this Part of the Act are contained in s.47 below.

See the General Notes to ss.38–48 for annotations of the individual provisions of those sections.

Management and investment of funds in court

38.—(1) Subject to rules made under subsection (7) below, all sums of money, securities and effects paid and deposited in, or under the custody of—

(*a*) the High Court;

(*b*) a county court; or

(*c*) such other courts and tribunals as the Lord Chancellor may by rules made under that subsection prescribe,

shall be vested in the Accountant General.

(2) One or more accounts shall be opened and kept in the name of the Accountant General at such bank or banks as may be designated by the Lord Chancellor with the concurrence of the Treasury.

(3) Money and securities held by the Accountant General shall vest in his successor in office without any assignment or transfer.

(4) A sum of money paid and deposited in court may, subject to subsection (5) below, be invested and reinvested by the Accountant General in any manner authorised by rules made under subsection (7) below.

(5) Where—

(*a*) a court orders that a particular fund in court shall be invested in a specified manner; and

(*b*) that manner is authorised by the rules referred to in subsection (7) below,

the Accountant General shall invest the fund in accordance with the order.

(6) The Accountant General may, in such cases as the Lord Chancellor may by rules made under subsection (7) below prescribe, apply to the court for an order for directions as to the manner in which a particular fund in court is to be dealt with.

(7) The Lord Chancellor, with the concurrence of the Treasury, may make provision as to the payment of interest on funds in court and may make rules as to the administration and management of funds in court including the deposit, payment, delivery and transfer in, into and out of any court of funds in court and regulating the evidence of such deposit, payment, delivery or transfer.

(8) Rules made under subsection (7) above may—

(*a*) provide for the discharge of the functions of the Accountant General under the rules by a person or persons appointed by him;

(*b*) provide for the transfer of money in court to and from the Commissioners;

(*c*) provide for money paid and deposited in a county court to be vested in, and accounted for by, a person other than the Accountant General;

(*d*) prescribe cases in which interest is to be paid on funds in court;

(*e*) prescribe cases in which funds in court are to be invested;

(*f*) make provision for the transfer of funds in court from one court to another; and

(*g*) prescribe cases in which moneys payable under a judgment or order shall be paid into court.

(9) Any such rules may make different provision for different cases.

GENERAL NOTE
Reference should be made to the General Note to this Part (VI) of the Act. This section was described in the explanatory memorandum to the Bill as dealing with the vesting of funds in court in the Accountant General, the relationship between him and the courts, and the general power to make rules concerning the administration and management of funds in court.

Investment of money transferred to National Debt Commissioners

39.—(1) The Commissioners may invest, in such manner as may be prescribed by regulations made by the Treasury, money transferred to them in pursuance of rules made under section 38(7) above or section 82(1) of the Judicature (Northern Ireland) Act 1978 and the interest or dividends accruing on investments made under this subsection.

(2) If in any accounting year the aggregate of the sums of money received by the Commissioners by way of interest and dividends on investments made by them under subsection (1) above, after deduction of—

    (*a*) any sum required by the Treasury to be set aside to provide for depreciation in the value of investments so made; and

    (*b*) such sum as the Lord Chancellor may with the concurrence of the Treasury direct to be paid to him in respect of the cost to him in that year of administering funds in court,

exceeds the aggregate of the sums due to be paid or credited in respect of that year by way of interest on funds in court, the excess shall be paid into the Consolidated Fund.

(3) If in any accounting year the aggregate of the sums of money received as mentioned in subsection (2) above, after deduction of the sum or sums falling to be deducted under paragraph (*a*) and (*b*) of that subsection, is less than the aggregate of the sums due as mentioned in that subsection, the deficiency shall be made good out of the Consolidated Fund.

(4) The Commissioners shall pay to the Lord Chancellor any sum deducted by them under subsection (2)(*b*) above; and any sum received by the Lord Chancellor under this subsection shall be paid into the Consolidated Fund.

(5) If at any time the Commissioners are unable to pay—

    (*a*) to the Accountant General a sum due from them to him under rules made under section 38(7) above; or

    (*b*) to the Accountant General of the Supreme Court of Judicature of Northern Ireland a sum due from them to him under rules made under section 82(1) of the Judicature (Northern Ireland) Act 1978,

the Treasury shall provide them with it out of the Consolidated Fund.

GENERAL NOTE
Reference should be made to the General Note to this Part (VI) of the Act. This section was described in the explanatory memorandum to the Bill as restating the current position relating to investment by the National Debt Commissioners of the funds moneys transferred to them.

Statutory deposits

40.—(1) Where money or securities are deposited with the Accountant General under any enactment or subordinate legislation, whether passed or made before or after the commencement of this Part of this Act, they shall for the purposes of this Part of this Act be treated as if they were funds in court except in so far as—

    (*a*) the enactment; or

    (*b*) the subordinate legislation; or

(*c*) rules made under section 38(7) above,
provide to the contrary.

(2) In subsection (1) above "subordinate legislation" means Orders in Council, orders, rules, regulations and other instruments made or to be made under any Act.

Transfer of funds in court to Official Custodian for Charities and Church Commissioners

41.—(1) Any funds for the time being vested in the Accountant General and held by him in trust for any charity or in trust for any ecclesiastical corporation in the Church of England may, if the Accountant General on an application made in that behalf to him by the Charity Commissioners or the Church Commissioners thinks fit so to direct, be transferred to the Official Custodian for Charities or the Church Commissioners, as the case may be.

(2) Any funds transferred by virtue of a direction given under subsection (1) above shall be vested in and held by the Official Custodian for Charities or the Church Commissioners respectively in trust for the charity or ecclesiastical corporation upon the trusts upon which the funds were held before the transfer.

(3) In this section "ecclesiastical corporation" means a capitular body within the meaning of the Cathedrals Measure 1963 or the incumbent of a benefice.

Common investment schemes

42.—(1) The Lord Chancellor may continue to make schemes ("common investment schemes") establishing common investment funds for the purpose of investing funds in court and money held by any person who in accordance with subsection (5)(*b*) below may hold shares in common investment funds.

(2) A common investment scheme shall provide for the fund thereby established to be under the management and control of an investment manager appointed by the Lord Chancellor.

(3) A common investment scheme shall make provision for the investment by its investment manager in accordance with the provisions of this section of funds in court transferred to the fund under rules made by virtue of section 38(7) above and of any sums of money transferred to the fund by persons who in accordance with subsection (5)(*b*) below may hold shares in the fund.

(4) A common investment scheme shall make provision—

 (*a*) for treating the fund established by it as being divided into shares; and

 (*b*) for treating a sum invested in the fund as being represented by a number of shares determined by reference to that sum and the value of the fund at the time the investment was made.

(5) Shares in a common investment fund—

(*a*) shall be allotted to and held by the Accountant General and

(*b*) may be allotted to and held by the Accountant General of the Supreme Court of Judicature of Northern Ireland and any other person authorised by the Lord Chancellor.

(6) Where a person is authorised under subsection (5) above to hold shares in a common investment fund—

(*a*) he shall have the same power to invest trust money in shares in the fund as if they were investments specified in Part I of Schedule 1 to the Trustee Investments Act 1961; and

(*b*) he may invest trust money in a common investment fund of which he is the investment manager.

(7) Moneys comprised in the fund established by a common investment scheme may, subject to the provisions of the scheme, be invested by the investment manager of the fund in any way in which he thinks fit, whether or not authorised by the general law in relation to trust funds.

(8) Neither the Prevention of Fraud (Investments) Act 1958 nor the Prevention of Fraud (Investments) Act (Northern Ireland) 1940 shall apply to dealings undertaken or documents issued for the purposes of a common investment scheme.

(9) The investment manager of a fund established by a common investment scheme shall not be required or entitled to take account of any trusts or equities affecting any share in the fund whether or not he is also a trustee of any such trust.

(10) The investment manager of a fund established by a common investment scheme shall be remunerated at such rates and in such manner as the Lord Chancellor shall with the concurrence of the Treasury determine.

(11) The salary or remuneration of an investment manager and his officers and such other expenses of executing his office or otherwise carrying this Part of this Act into effect as may be sanctioned by the Treasury shall be paid out of moneys provided by Parliament.

(12) There shall be charged in respect of the running of a common investment scheme such fees, whether by way of percentage or otherwise, as the Lord Chancellor shall with the concurrence of the Treasury fix and such fees shall be collected and accounted for by such persons, and in such manner, and shall be paid to such account, as the Treasury direct.

(13) There shall be retained or paid out of a fund established by a common investment scheme any expenses which could be so retained or paid out of trust property if the investment manager of the fund were a trustee and such expenses shall be retained or paid in the same way as and in addition to fees charged in respect of the running of the scheme.

(14) Fees and expenses recovered under this section shall be paid into the Consolidated Fund.

(15) Money and securities held by an investment manager of a fund established by a common investment scheme shall vest in his successor in office without any assignment or transfer.

(16) The power conferred by subsection (1) above to make a common investment scheme shall include the power to vary or revoke such a scheme.

GENERAL NOTE

The Lord Chancellor said of this clause in the Bill (*Hansard,* Vol. 428, col. 33) that it "will enable the Lord Chancellor to authorise persons other than the Accountant General to hold shares in the common investment schemes which are currently managed by the Public Trustee. In particular, it will permit the Public Trustee to hold shares in these funds, and therefore to make use of the benefits of these unitised investments on behalf of the trusts of which he is the trustee". The section also "reproduces the power to make common investment schemes to enable funds in court to benefit from conglomerate investment" (Explanatory Memorandum to the Bill).

This section is subject to the power of repeal or modification by Order in Council, contained in s.44 (below).

The General Note to this Part (VI) of the Act should also be consulted.

Provision for making good defaults

43. If the Lord Chancellor, whether on a recommendation made to him by any person interested or not, certifies—

(*a*) that the Accountant General; or

(*b*) that the manager of a common investment fund,

has been guilty of any default with respect to any money, securities and effects for which he is responsible under this Part of this Act, such sum as may be certified by the Lord Chancellor to be necessary for making good the default shall be paid out of moneys provided by Parliament or, if and so far as it is not so paid, shall be charged on and issued out of the Consolidated Fund.

GENERAL NOTE

The General Note to this Part (VI) of the Act should be consulted. This section provides for the making good of any default by the Accountant General or the manager of a common investment fund. The section is subject to the power of repeal or modification by Order in Council, contained in s.44, below.

Power to repeal and modify ss.42 and 43

44.—(1) Her Majesty may by Order in Council—

(*a*) repeal subsections (8), (10), (12), (14) and (15) of section 42 above and section 43 above; or

(*b*) make such modifications to those enactments as Her Majesty considers appropriate.

(2) Any Order in Council made under subsection (1) above shall be subject to annulment in pursuance of a resolution of either House of Parliament.

GENERAL NOTE

The General Note to this Part (VI) of the Act should be consulted.

Accounts

45.—(1) Accounts shall be prepared and shall at such times as the Treasury shall direct be sent to the Comptroller and Auditor General—

(*a*) in respect of his transactions under section 38 above, by the Accountant General;

(*b*) in respect of their transactions under section 39 above, by the Commissioners; and

(*c*) in respect of transactions in a fund established by a common investment scheme, by the investment manager.

(2) The accounts shall be in such form and shall be prepared in respect of such periods as the Treasury may direct.

(3) The Comptroller and Auditor General shall examine, certify and report on accounts sent to him under subsection (1) above and lay copies of them and his report on them before each House of Parliament.

GENERAL NOTE

The General Note to this Part (VI) of the Act should be consulted. This section provides for accounts in respect of transactions the subject of this Part of the Act.

Supplemental

46.—(1) Any power conferred by this Part of this Act to make a scheme or rules or regulations shall be exercisable by statutory instrument which shall be subject to annulment in pursuance of a resolution of either House of Parliament.

(2) The following amendments shall have effect—

(a) the words "invested under section 38 of the Administration of Justice Act 1982" shall be substituted for the words "dealt with under section 6 of the Administration of Justice Act 1965" in each case where they occur in the following enactments—

   (i) section 46 of the Chelsea and Kilmainham Hospitals Act 1826;

   (ii) section 12 of the ecclesiastical Houses of Residence Act 1842;

   (iii) sections 70, 78 and 86 of the Lands Clauses Consolidation Act 1845; and

   (iv) section 9 of the Tithe Act 1846;

(b) the words "section 42 of the Administration of Justice Act 1982" shall be substituted for the words "section 1 of the Administration of Justice Act 1965"—

   (i) in section $11(k)$ of the Light Railways Act 1896; and

   (ii) in section 20(1) of the Insurance Companies Act 1958;

(c) in section 7(1) of the Industrial Assurance Act 1923, for the words from the beginning of paragraph (a) to "1958" there shall be substituted—

   "(a) the provision substituted by the Administration of Justice Act 1965 for section 19(1) of the Insurance Companies Act 1958 and the provision so substituted for section 20(1) of that Act, as amended by section 46(2)(c) of the Administration of Justice Act 1982,";

(d) in Schedule 1 to the Administration of Justice Act 1965, in the entry relating to the Tramways Act 1870—

   (i) the words "of the Supreme Court" shall be inserted after the words "Accountant General" in the first and second place where they occur; and

   (ii) the words "under section 42 of the Administration of Justice Act 1982" shall be added after the words "common investment schemes";

(e) in section 413 of the Income and Corporation Taxes Act 1970—

   (i) in subsection (1), for the words from "section 1" to "Trustee", in the second place where it occurs, there shall be substituted the words "section 42 of the Administration of Justice Act 1982 is for the time being designated for the purposes of this subsection by an agreement between the Board and the investment manager of the fund—

      (a) the investment manager";

   (ii) in subsection (4), after the word "General" there shall be inserted the words "and any other person authorised to invest in a fund designated for the purposes of subsection (1) above"; and

   (iii) in subsection (5), for the words "Public Trustee" there shall be substituted the words "or the investment manager of the fund";

(f) in section 99(3) of the Capital Gains Tax 1979—

   (i) in paragraph (a), for the words "section 14 of the Administration of Justice Act 1965" there shall be substituted the words "section 40 of the Administration of Justice Act 1982"; and

   (ii) in paragraph (b) for the words from "any" to "Ireland", in the first place where it occurs, there shall be substituted the words "money in the Supreme Court of Judicature of Northern Ireland"; and

(g) in section 9(7) of the Insurance Companies Act 1981 for the words "section 7 of the Administration of Justice Act 1965" there shall be substituted the words "section 38(7) of the Administration of Justice Act 1982".

GENERAL NOTE

This section contains supplemental provisions, including amendments of legislation to give effect to the purposes of this Part (VI) of the Act, as to which see the General Note to this Part.

Interpretation

47. In this Part—

"Accountant General" means the Accountant General of the Supreme Court;

"the Commissioners" means the National Debt Commissioners;

"a common investment scheme" means a scheme made under section 42 above;

"funds" or "funds in court" means—

(a) any money, securities or other investments (including foreign currency and assets) standing or to be placed to the account—

(i) of the Accountant General by virtue of section 38(1) above; or

(ii) of any other person by virtue of rules made under subsection (7) of that section;

(b) any effects deposited with the Accountant General by virtue of section 38(1) above;

but does not include any statutory deposit referred to in section 40 above.

GENERAL NOTE

This section contains definitions of words and phrases used in this Part (VI) of the Act. See also the General Note to Pt. VI.

Application of Part VI to Scotland

48. This Part of this Act shall apply to Scotland only in relation to money or securities deposited with the Accountant General in the circumstances referred to in section 40 above; and in the application to Scotland of the power to make rules under section 38(7) above as to the payment or transfer out of court of money or securities treated, by virtue of section 40 above, as if, for the purposes of this Part of this Act, they were funds in court, for the reference to the Lord Chancellor there shall be substituted a reference to the Secretary of State.

GENERAL NOTE

See the General Note to this Part (VI) of the Act. It applies only to Scotland and enacts that this Part of the Act applies to Scotland only in relation to money or securities deposited with the Attorney General under s.40 above, *i.e.* under other legislation—see the General Note to that section.

PART VII

MISCELLANEOUS

Family law

Presentation of petitions for matrimonial relief on behalf of patients under Mental Health Act 1959

49. In section 103(1)(*h*) of the Mental Health Act 1959 the words from "so however" to the end of the paragraph (which prevent the Master of the Court of Protection and other officers of that Court making orders or giving directions or authorities to present petitions for matrimonial relief in the name or on behalf of patients) shall cease to have effect.

GENERAL NOTE

This section comes into operation on January 1, 1983 (s.76(11)). It equates the presentation of petitions for divorce, nullity, or judicial separation by patients with other proceedings by ceasing to require the authority of the Lord Chancellor or of a nominated judge for the presentation of such petitions. The Master of the Court of Protection can now, for example, give such authority (as to a Deputy Master, see s.60 below).

Orders for the maintenance of wards of court

50. In section 6(2)(*b*) of the Family Law Reform Act 1969 (which empowers the High Court to make an order requiring parents of a ward of court to make periodical payments towards the maintenance and education of the ward) after the words "the ward" there shall be inserted the words "or to the ward".

GENERAL NOTE

This section comes into operation on January 1, 1983 (s.76(11)). It empowers the High Court to order either or both parents to make periodical payments (towards the maintenance and education of the ward) to the ward of court personally as an alternative to payment to a person having care and control of the ward.

Remission of arrears of maintenance

51. The following subsection shall be inserted after subsection (2) of section 31 of the Matrimonial Causes Act 1973 (which gives the High Court and divorce county courts power to vary or discharge certain orders for the payment of maintenance, etc. or to suspend any provision thereof temporarily and to revive the operation of any provision so suspended)—

"(2A) Where the court has made an order referred to in subsection (2)(*a*), (*b*) or (*c*) above, then, subject to the provisions of this section, the court shall have power to remit the payment of any arrears due under the order or of any part thereof.".

GENERAL NOTE

This section comes into operation on January 1, 1983 (s.76(11)). It was described by the explanatory memorandum to the Bill as giving the divorce courts substantially the same powers as magistrates' courts to remit arrears of maintenance. The orders referred to in s.31(2)(*a*), (*b*), and (*c*) of the Matrimonial Causes Act 1973 are (*a*) any order for maintenance pending suit; (*b*) any periodical payments order; and (*c*) any secured periodical payments order.

Filing of orders

52. In section 19(3) of the Inheritance (Provision for Family and Dependants) Act 1975 (under which a copy of every order made under the Act is to be sent to the principal registry of the Family Division for entry and filing, and a memorandum of the order is to be endorsed on, or permanently annexed to, the probate or letters of administration under which the estate is being administered) after the words "made under this Act" there shall be inserted the words "other than an order made under section 15(1) of this Act".

GENERAL NOTE
This section comes into operation on the day the Act was passed (s.76(9) and (10)), namely October 28, 1982. The section exempts from the requirement of filing of orders (and noting on the grant of representation) orders made under s.15(1) of the Inheritance (Provision for Family and Dependants) Act 1975, *i.e.* orders on a decree of divorce, nullity, or judicial separation that either party to the marriage shall not be entitled, on the death of the other party, to apply for an order for financial provision under the 1975 Act.

Amendments of Attachment of Earnings Act 1971

Power to order debtor to appear before court where attachment of earnings order is in force

53.—(1) In section 14(2) of the Attachment of Earnings Act 1971 (power of court to make certain orders where an attachment of earnings order is in force) for the words from "make such" to the end there shall be substituted the words—

"(*a*) make such an order as is described in subsection (1)(*a*) or (*b*) above; and

(*b*) order the debtor to attend before it on a day and at a time specified in the order to give the information described in subsection (1)(*a*) above.".

(2) In section 23(1) of that Act (enforcement provisions)—

(*a*) after the words "an order" there shall be inserted the words "or with an order made under section 14(2)(*b*) above"; and

(*b*) after the words "hearing of the application" there shall be inserted the words "or specified in the order".

GENERAL NOTE
This section comes into operation on January 1, 1983 (s.76(11)). The section gives the Court (High Court, county court, or magistrates' court) power to order the debtor to attend before it to give particulars of his employer, earnings, resources, needs, etc. (s.14(1)(*a*), (*b*) of the Attachment of Earnings Act 1971). Moreover, in a county court case, the judge's power to order the imprisonment of the debtor for up to 14 days (1971 Act, s.23(1)) is extended to non-compliance with an order to attend and give the above information.

Deductions by employer under attachment of earnings order

54. The following paragraph shall be substituted for paragraph 4 of Schedule 3 to the Attachment of Earnings Act 1971 (deductions by employer under attachment of earnings order)—

"4.—(1) On any pay-day—

(*a*) "the normal deduction" is arrived at by applying the normal deduction rate (as specified in the relevant attachment of earnings order) with respect to the relevant period; and

(*b*) "the protected earnings" are arrived at by applying the protected earnings rate (as so specified) with respect to the relevant period.

(2) For the purposes of this paragraph the relevant period in relation to any pay-day is the period beginning—

(*a*) if it is the first pay-day of the debtor's employment with the employer, with the first day of the employment; or

(*b*) if on the last pay-day earnings were paid in respect of a

period falling wholly or partly after that pay-day, with
the first day after the end of that period; or
(*c*) in any other case, with the first day after the last pay-day,
and ending—
    (i) where earnings are paid in respect of a period
falling wholly or partly after the pay-day, with the
last day of that period; or
    (ii) in any other case, with the pay-day.".

GENERAL NOTE
  This section comes into operation on such day as the Lord Chancellor may appoint
(s.76(1), (2)). It enlarges the rules contained in para. 4 of Sched. 3 to the Attachment of
Earnings Act 1971 by allowing deduction in respect of earnings paid in advance, for example
holiday pay (new para. 4(2)(*b*)).

Attachment of debts

Attachment of debts

  55.—(1) The section set out in Part I of Schedule 4 to this Act shall be
inserted after section 40 of the Supreme Court Act 1981.
  (2) The section set out in Part II of that Schedule shall be inserted after
section 143 of the County Courts Act 1959.

GENERAL NOTE
  This section comes into operation on January 1, 1983 (s.76(11)). It inserts (by reference
to Sched. 4) new sections in the Supreme Court Act 1981 and the County Courts Act 1959
to allow orders to prescribe administrative and clerical expenses that may be deducted by
deposit-taking institutions such as banks (see s.40 of the 1981 Act) from credit balances,
etc., held on behalf of judgment debtors, when those balances are attached (garnisheed) by
order of the Court in enforcement of the judgment. No such deduction is to be permitted
if the debtor is bankrupt or, being a company, is in liquidation (for details see s.40 of the
Bankruptcy Act 1914, and s.325 of the Companies Act 1948).

Penalties under Solicitors Act 1974

Increase in penalty etc.

  56.—In section 47 of the Solicitors Act 1974 (powers of Solicitors
Disciplinary Tribunal)—
  (*a*) in subsection (2)(*c*) (payment by solicitor of penalty) for "£750"
there shall be substituted "£3,000"; and
  (*b*) the following subsections shall be added after subsection (3)—
    "(4) If it appears to the Lord Chancellor that there has been
a change in the value of money since the relevant date, he may
by order made by statutory instrument subject to annulment in
pursuance of a resolution of either House of Parliament sub-
situte for the sum for the time being specified in subsection
(2)(*c*) above such other sum as appears to him to be justified
by the change.
    (5) In subsection (4) above "the relevant date" means—
      (*a*) in relation to the first order under that subsection,
the date of the coming into force of section 56 of
the Administration of Justice Act 1982; and
      (*b*) in relation to each subsequent order, the last
occasion when the sum specified in subsection
(2)(*c*) above was altered.".

GENERAL NOTE
  This section comes into operation on January 1, 1983 (s.76(11)). It empowers the Solicitors
Disciplinary Tribunal (constituted under s.46 of the Solicitors Act 1974, c.47), when imposing
a penalty on a solicitor under s.47(2)(*c*) of the 1974 Act, to impose a maximum of £3,000 (or

such a sum as shall be prescribed by order—see the new subss.(4), (5) of s.47 of the 1974 Act, inserted by the present section) instead of the present maximum of £750.

Judicial Trustees

Accounts of judicial trustees

57.—(1) In section 1(6) of the Judicial Trustees Act 1896 (by virtue of which, among other things, the accounts of every trust of which a judicial trustee has been appointed have to be audited once in every year, and a report on them made to the court) the words from the beginning to "and", in the second place where it occurs, shall cease to have effect.

(2) The following paragraphs shall be substituted for paragraph (11) of subsection (1) of section 4 of that Act (by virtue of which rules may be made for the filing and auditing of the accounts of any trust of which a judicial trustee has been appointed)—

"(11) for the preparation, auditing (by the court or otherwise) and filing of the accounts of any trust of which a judicial trustee has been appointed;

(12) for the making of a report to the court on the accounts of any such trust.".

(3) The following subsection shall be inserted after the said subsection (1)—

"(1A) The rules under this Act may make different provision for different classes of trust, trustees, beneficiaries or trust property.".

GENERAL NOTE

This section comes into operation on such day as the Lord Chancellor shall by order appoint (s.76(1), (2)). It was described by the explanatory memorandum to the Bill as making auditing of the accounts of a judicial trustee a matter for rules rather than substantive law. Ss.1, 4 of the Judicial Trustees Act 1896 (c.35) are amended accordingly. It implements a recommendation of the Oliver Report on Practice and Procedure in the Chancery Division (Cmnd. 8205).

Recorders

Assistance by Recorders for transaction of business of High Court

58. At the end of the Table in section 9(1) of the Supreme Court Act 1981 (under which certain persons may be requested to act as judges in specified courts) there shall be added—

"6. A Recorder.   The High Court".

GENERAL NOTE

This section comes into operation on January 1, 1983 (s.76(11)). It provides that the Lord Chancellor's power to request holders of specified judicial office to act as a judge in the High Court (under s.9(1) of the Supreme Court Act 1981) be extended to a request to a Recorder (including Solicitor Recorders). It regularises the practice prior to the 1981 Act (see *Hansard*, H.L. Vol. 435, cols. 569–70).

Official referees' business

Official referees' business

59.—(1) In subsection (1)(*a*) of section 68 of the Supreme Court Act 1981 (by virtue of which the Lord Chancellor may nominate Circuit judges to deal with official referees' business) for the words "of the Circuit judges" there shall be substituted the words "Circuit judges, deputy Circuit judges or Recorders".

(2) Accordingly—

(*a*) the word "persons" shall be substituted—

(i) for the words "Circuit judges" in subsections (5) and (6) of that section; and

(ii) for the word "judges", in the second place where it occurs in subsection (6); and

(b) the word "person" shall be substituted for the words "Circuit judge" in subsection (7).

(3) In subsection (4) of section 24 of the Courts Act 1971 (deputy Circuit judges and assistant Recorders) for the words "as regards any" there shall be substituted the words "in the case of a deputy Circuit judge, as regards".

GENERAL NOTE

This section comes into operation on January 1, 1983 (s.76(11)). It amends s.68 of the Supreme Court Act 1981 to enable a deputy Circuit Judge and a Recorder (including a Solicitor) to be appointed as an Official Referee, to try for example, lengthy building disputes.

Deputy Master of Court of Protection

Power to abolish office of Deputy Master of Court of Protection

60. In section 89(6) of the Supreme Court Act 1981 after the words "Chancery Division" there shall be inserted the words "and the office of Deputy Master of the Court of Protection".

GENERAL NOTE

This section came into operation on the day the Act was passed (s.76(10)), *i.e.* October 28, 1982. It enables the Lord Chancellor by order to abolish the office of Deputy Master of the Court of Protection.

Jurors

Questions to persons summoned for jury service

61. In section 2(5) of the Juries Act 1974—

(a) for the words "attend in pursuance of such a summons, or of a summons" there shall be substituted the words "is summoned under subsection (4) above or"; and

(b) after the word "may", in the second place where it occurs, there shall be inserted the words "at any time".

GENERAL NOTE

This section comes into operation on January 1, 1983 (s.76(11)). Its purpose was described as follows by the Lord Chancellor (*Hansard*, H.L., Vol. 435, col. 572):

"The purpose [of this section] is to ensure that questions may be put to a prospective juror to ascertain whether he is qualified for jury service at any time and not just when he attends in pursuance of a jury summons. The result will be that if a juror refuses without reasonable excuse to answer, or knowingly or recklessly gives a false answer to the questions which are customarily set out in the jury summons, he will commit an offence which is at present triable summarily before magistrates with a maximum fine at present of £100, though under the Criminal Justice Bill it will be a maximum of £200."

This applies equally to a juror who pretends to have a disqualification which he does not have in order to try to avoid jury service. (*Ibid.*, *per* Lord Mishcon).

Inquests

Juries where death in police custody, etc. suspected

62. In section 13(2) of the Coroners (Amendment) Act 1926 (which requires a coroner to summon a jury in certain circumstances) there shall be added after paragraph (*e*) the following paragraph—

"or

(*f*) that the death occurred while the deceased was in police custody, or resulted from an injury caused by a police officer in the purported execution of his duty;".

GENERAL NOTE

This section comes into operation on January 1, 1983 (s.76(11)). It amends s.13(2) of the Coroners (Amendment) Act 1926, which requires a coroner to summon a jury when there is reason to suspect specified circumstances, to extend that requirement to cases where the deceased was in police custody, or death resulted from an injury caused by a police officer in the purported execution of his duty.

Explosive substances—consents to prosecutions

Consents to prosecutions under the Explosive Substances Act 1883

63.—(1) The following subsection shall be substituted for section 7(1) of the Explosive Substances Act 1883—

"(1) Proceedings for a crime under this Act shall not be instituted except by or with the consent of the Attorney General.".

(2) In section 9(2) of that Act (application to Scotland) the following paragraph shall be inserted before the paragraph relating to the expression "Attorney General"—

"Section 7(1) shall be omitted."

GENERAL NOTE

This section comes into operation on January 1, 1983 (s.76(11)). It simplifies the procedure for the Attorney General giving his consent to a prosecution under the Explosives Act 1883. See the explanation of the procedural difficulties given by Lord Mishcon, *Hansard*, H.L., Vol. 435, col. 574, where he pointed out that under the existing procedure the charge had to be brought first by the Director of Public Prosecutions before the magistrate(s) before the Attorney General's *fiat* was asked for. Now, the D.P.P. will simply apply for the Attorney General's *fiat* before commencing proceedings.

Constitution of the Law Commission

Temporary vacancies in Law Commission

64. In section 1(1) of the Law Commissions Act 1965 (by virtue of which the Law Commission consists of a Chairman and four other Commissioners) after the word "consisting" there shall be inserted the words "(except during any temporary vacancy)".

GENERAL NOTE

This section came into operation on the day that the Act was passed (s.76(9)(10)), *i.e.* October 28, 1982. It preserves the quorum of the Law Commission where the statutory composition is not present because of a temporary vacancy.

Justices of the Peace

Appointment of justices of the peace

65. In section 6(1) of the Justices of the Peace Act 1979 for the words from "on behalf" to "Chancellor" there shall be substituted the words "by the Lord Chancellor by instrument on behalf and in the name of Her Majesty".

GENERAL NOTE

This section came into operation on the day that the Act was passed (s.76(9), (10)), *i.e.* October 28, 1982. It removes the requirement of s.6(1) of the Justices of the Peace Act 1979 that the appointment or removal of a justice of the peace must be under the Lord Chancellor's *hand*.

Land Registration

Computerisation of the title register

66.—(1) The following section shall be substituted for section 1 of the Land Registration Act 1925—

"Registers to be continued
    1.—(1) The Chief Land Registrar shall continue to keep a register of title to freehold land and leasehold land.
    (2) The register need not be kept in documentary form.".

(2) The following section shall be inserted after section 113 of that Act—

"Inspection etc.—supplementary
    113A.—(1) Any duty under this Act to make a thing available for inspection is a duty to make it available for inspection in visible and legible form.
    (2) Any reference in this Act to copies of and extracts from the register and of and from documents and plans filed in the registry includes a reference to reproductions of things which are kept by the registrar under this Act otherwise than in documentary form.".

GENERAL NOTE
    This section comes into operation on January 1, 1983 (s.76(11)). Its purpose is to facilitate computerisation of the Land Register, by allowing the register to be kept "otherwise than in documentary form" and copies to be supplied of a register so kept.

Jurisdiction

67.—(1) The Land Registration Act 1925 shall have effect subject to the amendments specified in Schedule 5 to this Act.
    (2) The Land Registration Rules 1967 are revoked.

GENERAL NOTE
    This section and Sched. 5 to which it refers comes into operation on January 1, 1983 (s.76(11)). It was stated by the Lord Chancellor (*Hansard*, H.L., Vol. 428, col. 33) simply to clarify the powers of the county courts under the land registration legislation and not to make any changes of substance. This is done by appropriate amendments to the Land Registration Act 1925, and the Land Registration Rules 1967, S.I. 1967 No. 761, are consequently revoked.

PART VIII

PROVISIONS RELATING TO NORTHERN IRELAND

GENERAL NOTE
    This part of the Act relates only to Northern Ireland. The Lord Chancellor said of this Part, when introducing the Bill in the House of Lords (*Hansard*, H.L., Vol. 428, col. 33), that almost all its provisions were intended to keep Northern Ireland in step with changes in the law in England and Wales. In particular the changes in Sched. 6 ensure that changes in the law regarding personal injury litigation proceed at an even pace in the two "countries." Almost all the changes in Sched. 7 reflect provisions in the law of England and Wales which are to be found either in Pts. VI or VII of this Act or in the Supreme Court Act 1981, ss.71 and 72, as to expert evidence and allowances for justices of the peace respectively are modelled on provisions in the law of England and Wales (see below).

Damages for personal injuries etc.

68. Schedule 6 to this Act shall have effect.

This section comes into operation on January 1, 1983 (s.76(11)) and by Sched. 6, applies the changes in the law as to damages for personal injuries, etc., contained for England and Wales in Pt. I (ss.1–6) of this Act. The General Notes to ss.1–6 above should therefore be consulted for detailed annotations, relevant to the provisions of Sched. 6. S.73(1)(2), (4)(*c*) of this Act contains transitional provisions (similar to these for England and Wales) as to the provisions of Sched. 6 relating to damages for personal injuries, and a special transitional provision is contained in s.73(9) for actions for enticement, etc., in Northern Ireland.

Interest on debts and damages

69.—(1) The section set out in Part I of Schedule 7 to this Act shall be inserted after section 33 of the Judicature (Northern Ireland) Act 1978.

(2) The Article set out in Part II of that Schedule shall be inserted after Article 45 of the County Courts (Northern Ireland) Order 1980.

(3) The enactments specified in Part III of that Schedule shall have effect subject to the amendments there specified being amendments consequential on subsections (1) and (2) above.

This section comes into operation on such day as the Lord Chancellor may by order appoint (s.76(1), (2)). This section, by reference to Sched. 7, applies to Northern Ireland the amendments in the law as to interest on debts and damages contained, for England and Wales, in s.15 of and Sched. 1 to this Act, the General Notes to which should therefore be consulted.

Amendments of Judicature (Northern Ireland) Act 1978

70. The Judicature (Northern Ireland) Act 1978 shall have effect subject to the amendments specified in Schedule 8 to this Act.

This section comes into operation on January 1, 1983 (s.76(11)). It amends the Judicature (Northern Ireland) Act 1978 by reference to Sched. 8. That Schedule contains (i) provisions applicable only to Northern Ireland, for example, paras. 1 and 2 relating to the Court of Appeal in Northern Ireland and to judicial oaths; (ii) provisions equivalent to sections of this Act applicable to England and Wales, for example, para. 3 corresponding to s.50 (payments to wards of court) and paras. 6–8 corresponding to Pt. VI of the Act; and (iii) provisions corresponding to provisions of the Supreme Court Act 1981 for example, para 10 (injunctions restraining removal of assets from the jurisdiction), corresponding to s.37(3) of the 1981 Act, and para 11, relating to the withdrawal of privilege against incrimination of self or spouse in certain proceedings corresponding to s.72 of the 1981 Act.

Rules of court with respect to expert reports and oral expert evidence

71.—(1) Notwithstanding any enactment or rule of law by virtue of which documents prepared for the purpose of pending or contemplated civil proceedings or in connection with the obtaining or giving of legal advice are in certain circumstances privileged from disclosure, provision may be made by rules of court for enabling the court in any civil proceedings to direct, with respect to medical matters or matters of any other class which may be specified in the direction, that the parties or some of them shall each by such date as may be so specified (or such later date as may be permitted or agreed in accordance with the rules) disclose to the other or others in the form of one or more expert reports the expert evidence on matters of that class which he proposes to adduce as part of his case at the trial.

(2) Provision may be made by rules of court as to the conditions subject to which oral expert evidence may be given in civil proceedings.

(3) Without prejudice to the generality of subsection (2), rules of court made in pursuance of that subsection may make provision for prohibiting a party who fails to comply with a direction given by virtue of rules under

subsection (1) from adducing, except with the leave of the court, any oral expert evidence whatsoever with respect to matters of any class specified in the direction.

(4) Any rules of court made in pursuance of this section may make different provision for different classes of cases, for expert reports dealing with matters of different classes, and for other different circumstances.

(5) References in this section to an expert report are references to a written report by a person dealing wholly or mainly with matters on which he is (or would if living be) qualified to give expert evidence.

(6) In this section "rules of court" means—

(a) rules of court made under section 55 of the Judicature (Northern Ireland) Act 1978; and

(b) county court rules made under Article 47 of the County Courts (Northern Ireland) Order 1980;

and nothing in this section shall prejudice the generality of the said section 55 and Article 47.

GENERAL NOTE
   This section comes into operation on January 1, 1983 (s.76(11)). It introduces into the law of Northern Ireland provisions akin to those contained, for England and Wales, in the Rules of the Supreme Court, Order 38, rules 37, 38, and 39. The annotations to those rules in the Annual Practice (the "White Book") should prove helpful in construing this section and rules made thereunder.

Travelling, subsistence and financial loss allowances for justices of the peace

72.—(1) The following section shall be inserted after section 12 of the Magistrates' Courts Act (Northern Ireland) 1964—

"Travelling, subsistence and financial loss allowances for justices of the peace

12A.—(1) Subject to the provisions of this section, a justice of the peace other than a resident magistrate shall be entitled—

(a) to receive payments by way of travelling allowance or subsistence allowance where expenditure on travelling or, as the case may be, on subsistence is necessarily incurred by him for the purpose of enabling him to perform any of his duties as a justice, and

(b) to receive payments by way of financial loss allowance where for that performance there is incurred by him any other expenditure to which he would not otherwise be subject or there is suffered by him any loss of earnings or of benefit under the enactments relating to social security which he would otherwise have made or received.

(2) Allowances under this section shall be paid at rates determined by the Lord Chancellor with the consent of the Treasury.".

(2) Sums required for the purposes of the section inserted in the Magistrates' Courts Act (Northern Ireland) 1964 by subsection (1) above shall be paid out of money provided by Parliament.

GENERAL NOTE
   This section comes into operation on January 1, 1983 (s.76(11)). It introduces into the Law of Northern Ireland provisions akin to those contained, for England and Wales, in s.12 of the Justices of the Peace Act 1979.

PART IX

GENERAL AND SUPPLEMENTARY

Transitional provisions and savings

73.—(1) Subject to subsections (2) and (3) below, nothing in Part I of this Act or paragraphs 2 to 10 of Schedule 6 to this Act applies to causes of action which accrue before its commencement.

(2) Section 6 above and paragraph 10 of Schedule 6 to this Act shall apply to actions whenever commenced, including actions commenced before the passing of this Act.

(3) The provisions to which this subsection applies have effect where a person has died after the commencement of Part I of this Act.

(4) The provisions of this Act to which subsection (3) above applies are—

   (*a*) section 1;

   (*b*) section 4(2); and

   (*c*) paragraph 9(2) of Schedule 6.

(5) Without prejudice to the provisions of Parts II and III of the Prescription and Limitation (Scotland) Act 1973, Part II of this Act shall apply to rights of action which accrued before, as well as rights of action which accrue after, the coming into operation of that Part of this Act; but nothing in Part II of this Act other than the repeal of section 5 of the Damages (Scotland) Act 1976 shall affect any proceedings commenced before that Part of this Act comes into operation.

(6) Nothing in the following provisions of this Act—

   (*a*) section 17;

   (*b*) section 18(2);

   (*c*) sections 19 to 22;

   (*d*) section 75, so far as it relates—

      (i) to the Wills Act Amendment Act 1852; and

      (ii) to the Family Law Reform Act 1969,

affects the will of a testator who dies before the commencement of the provision in question.

(7) Neither section 18(1) above nor the repeal by this Act of section 177 of the Law of Property Act 1925 affects a will made before the commencement of section 18(1) above.

(8) Until Part VI of this Act comes into force—

   (*a*) in section 1 of the Administration of Justice Act 1965—

      (i) in subsection (4), after the word "General" there shall be inserted the words "and the Public Trustee"; and

      (ii) the following subsection shall be inserted after that subsection—

        "(4A) Where provision is made by a common investment scheme for the Public Trustee to hold shares in a common investment fund, he shall have the same power to invest trust money in shares in the fund as if they were investments specified in Part I of Schedule 1 to the Trustee Investments Act 1961."; and

   (*b*) in the County Courts Act 1959—

      (i) the following subsection shall be substituted for section 99(3)—

        "(3) Subject to rules under section 168 of this Act, all moneys payable under a judgment or order shall be paid into court."; and

      (ii) the following paragraph shall be added at the end of section 168—

"(*o*) prescribing cases in which moneys payable under a judgment or order are to be paid by one party to the other party or his solicitor and regulating, in such cases as may be prescribed, the evidence of such payment.".

(9) Nothing in paragraph 1 of Schedule 6 to this Act affects a cause of action accruing before that paragraph comes into force if an action in respect thereof has been begun before the paragraph comes into force.

GENERAL NOTE

This section, except subs. (8), comes into operation on January 1, 1983 (s.76(11)). Subs. (8) comes into operation on such day as the Lord Chancellor appoints by order (s.76(2)). It contains transitional provisions and savings, the effect of which is included in the annotations to the individual sections or schedules affected, unless specific annotations are given below.

Subs. (5): The subsection draws a distinction between (a) rights of action accruing, and (b) proceedings commenced, before Pt. II of the Act comes into operation. (See the note to s.14(2) as to the repeal of s.5 of the Damages (Scotland) Act 1976.) This repeal apart, nothing in Pt. II affects proceedings commenced before it comes into operation. By contrast Pt. II does apply to rights of action accruing before this, together with rights accruing after, though without prejudice to the provisions of Pt. II and III of the Prescription and Limitation (Scotland) Act 1973, which relate to the limitation of actions and the extension of time limits.

The insertion of the provision as to the repeal of s.5 of the 1976 Act is the result of an amendment agreed to in committee in the House of Lords (see H.L., April 6, 1982, col. 207). The new rules of court replacing s.5 come into operation when the present Act itself does even in relation to actions in progress and started on the basis of s.5. The usual rule that actions already in progress should be completed under the old law seeming inappropriate, provision is made for the repeal to be taken into account.—(See also s.14(3).)

Subs. (8): This subsection contains amendments to the Administration of Justice Act 1965 and the County Courts Act 1959, the effect of which is indicated below, to operate until Pt. VI of the Act (relating to Funds in Court) is brought into operation by appropriate Commencement Order(s) (see the General Note to Pt. VI, above).

Subs. (8)(a)(i): S.1(4) of the Administration of Justice Act 1965 provides:

"A common investment scheme shall make provision for the allotment of the shares into which the fund thereby established is divided to, and their holding by, the Accountant General [and the Public Trustee], but no other person."

The effect of this part of subs. (8) is to add the words "and the Public Trustee", where indicated in square brackets.

Subs. (8)(a)(ii): This should be compared with the General Note to s.46, above.

Subs. (8)(b): The existing s.99(3) of the County Courts Act 1959 provides simply that all moneys payable under a judgment or order shall be paid into court, without any reference to rules under s.168 of the 1959 Act. However, s.99(3) adds, "[p]rovided that where no order is made as to payment by instalments, the money shall, if the court so directs, be paid by one party to the other party or his solicitor subject to the lien, if any, of that solicitor." That proviso is not contained in the s.99(3) substituted by this part of the present subsection, the question of payment to a party or his solicitor to be the subject of rules made under the new paragraph (*o*) of s.168 of the 1959 Act (s.73(8)(*b*)(ii) of this Act).

Interest on damages—disregard for income tax purposes

74. In section 375A of the Income and Corporation Taxes Act 1970 (interest on damages for personal injuries or death not income for income tax purposes)—

(*a*) in paragraph (*a*) of subsection (1), for the words from "an order" to "1937" there shall be substituted the words "a provision to which this paragraph applies"; and

(*b*) the following subsection shall be inserted after subsection (1A) of that section—

"(1B) The provisions to which subsection (1)(*a*) of this section applies are—

(*a*) section 3 of the Law Reform (Miscellaneous Provisions) Act 1934;

(*b*) section 17 of the Law Reform (Miscellaneous Provisions) Act (Northern Ireland) 1937;
(*c*) section 35A of the Supreme Court Act 1981;
(*d*) section 97A of the County Courts Act 1959;
(*e*) section 33A of the Judicature (Northern Ireland) Act 1978; and
(*f*) Article 45A of the County Courts (Northern Ireland) Order 1980.".

GENERAL NOTE
This section comes into operation on January 1, 1983 (s.76(11)). It alters the law (as laid down in *Riches* v. *Westminster Bank* [1947] A.C. 390), by exempting from income tax, interest on debts or damages awarded under the statutory provisions listed in subs.(*b*) of this section. Those provisions (as amended or introduced by this Act) relate to the new power of the courts to award interest on debts or damages contained in Sched. 1 to this Act and to existing powers of awarding interest—see the General Notes to s.15 and Sched. 1 of this Act.

Repeals and revocations

75.—(1) The enactments specified in Part I of Schedule 9 to this Act (which include enactments already obsolete or unnecessary) are repealed to the extent specified in the third column of that Part of that Schedule.

(2) The instruments specified in Part II of that Schedule are revoked to the extent specified in the third column of that Part of that Schedule.

GENERAL NOTE
This section (save as below) comes into operation on January 1, 1983 (s.76(11)) but not until appropriate commencement order(s) in the cases set out in s.76(2)(i), (4)(*d*), (6)(*c*), below. It contains, by reference to Sched. 9, repeals of Acts and revocations of statutory instruments. It should also be borne in mind that this Act contains numerous substitutions of sections in existing Acts (for example, ss.1–4 in the Fatal Accidents Act 1976 by s.3 of this Act) which have the effect of repealing the original sections but do not necessarily appear in Sched. 9.
The repeal of s.177 of the Law of Property Act 1925 does not affect a will made before January 1, 1983 (s.73(7)). The repeal of the Wills Act Amendment Act 1852 does not affect the will of a testator who dies before January 1, 1983 (s.73(6)) nor does the repeal extend to Northern Ireland (s.77(5)). The repeal of s.16 of the Family Law Reform Act 1969 (c.46) does not affect the will of a testator who dies before January 1, 1983 (s.73(6)).

Commencement

76.—(1) The provisions of this Act specified in subsection (2) below shall come into operation on such day as the Lord Chancellor may by order appoint.

(2) The provisions of this Act mentioned in subsection (1) above are—
(*a*) section 6;
(*b*) Part III;
(*c*) sections 34 and 35;
(*d*) sections 38 to 47;
(*e*) section 54;
(*f*) section 57;
(*g*) section 69;
(*h*) section 73(8);
(*j*) section 75, so far as it relates—
  (i) to the Judicial Trustees Act 1896;
  (ii) to section 17 of the Law Reform (Miscellaneous Provisions) Act (Northern Ireland) 1937;
  (iii) to the Prevention of Fraud (Investments) Act 1958;

    (iv) to sections 99(3), 168 to 174A and 176 of the County Courts Act 1959;

    (v) to sections 1 to 16 of the Administration of Justice Act 1965 and Schedule 1 to that Act;

    (vi) to the Administration of Justice Act 1977; and

    (vii) to the Judicature (Northern Ireland) Act 1978;

  (*k*) paragraph 10 of the Schedule 6; and

  (*l*) paragraphs 6 to 8 of Schedule 8.

(3) The provisions of this Act specified in subsection (4) below shall come into operation on such day as the Secretary of State may by order appoint.

(4) The provisions of this Act mentioned in subsection (3) above are—

  (*a*) section 12;

  (*b*) section 14(2);

  (*c*) section 48; and

  (*d*) section 75 above, so far as it relates to the damages (Scotland) Act 1976.

(5) The provisions of this Act specified in subsection (6) below shall come into operation on such day as the Lord Chancellor and the Secretary of State may by order jointly appoint.

(6) The provisions of this Act mentioned in subsection (5) above are—

  (*a*) sections 23 to 25;

  (*b*) sections 27 and 28;

  (*c*) section 75, so far as it relates—

    (i) to section 126 of the Supreme Court Act 1981; and

    (ii) to Article 27 of the Administration of Estates (Northern Ireland) Order 1979.

(7) Any order under this section shall be made by statutory instrument.

(8) Any such order may appoint different days for different provisions and for different purposes.

(9) The provisions of this Act specified in subsection (10) below shall come into operation on the day this Act is passed.

(10) The provisions of this Act mentioned in subsection (9) above are—

  (*a*) section 32;

  (*b*) section 36;

  (*c*) section 52;

  (*d*) section 60;

  (*e*) section 64;

  (*f*) section 65;

  (*g*) this section;

  (*h*) section 77; and

  (*j*) section 78.

(11) Subject to the foregoing provisions of this section, this Act shall come into operation on 1st January 1983.

GENERAL NOTE

  This section came into operation on the day the Act was passed (subss. (9), (10)), *i.e.,* October 28, 1982. It contains provisions as to commencement of the sections of this Act, which are set out in the annotations to those sections. At the time of going to press, no commencement orders had been made under subss. (1), (3), or (5).

Extent

77.—(1) Subject to subsection (6) below, the following provisions of this Act—

  (*a*) sections 3, 4 and 6;

(*b*) Part III;
(*c*) sections 17 to 22;
(*d*) Part V;
(*e*) sections 49 to 57;
(*f*) sections 65 to 67,
extend to England and Wales only.

(2) Sections 1, 2, 5, 39, 42 to 47, 64 and 74 above extend to England and Wales and Northern Ireland.

(3) Part II of this Act and section 26 above extend to Scotland only and Part VI of this Act applies to Scotland only to the extent specified in section 48 above.

(4) Part VIII of this Act extends to Northern Ireland only.

(5) The repeal of the Wills Act Amendment Act 1852 by section 75 above does not extend to Northern Ireland.

(6) Subject to subsection (5) above, where any enactment repealed or amended or instrument revoked by this Act extends to any part of the United Kingdom, the repeal, amendment of revocation extends to that part.

GENERAL NOTE

This section came into operation on the day the Act was passed (s.76(9), (10)), *i.e.* October 28, 1982. It concerns the extent to which the provisions of this Act apply to England and Wales, Scotland, and Northern Ireland and its effect is set out under the head "extent" in the General Note to the whole Act, above.

Citation

78. This Act may be cited as the Administration of Justice Act 1982.

SCHEDULES

Section 15   SCHEDULE 1

INTEREST ON DEBTS AND DAMAGES

PART I

SECTION INSERTED IN SUPREME COURT ACT 1981

Power of High Court to award interest on debts and damages

35A.—(1) Subject to rules of court, in proceedings (whenever instituted) before the High Court for the recovery of a debt or damages there may be included in any sum for which judgment is given simple interest, at such rate as the court thinks fit or as rules of court may provide, on all or any part of the debt or damages in respect of which judgment is given, or payment is made before judgment, for all or any part of the period between the date when the cause of action arose and—

(*a*) in the case of any sum paid before judgment, the date of the payment; and

(*b*) in the case of the sum for which judgment is given, the date of the judgment.

(2) In relation to a judgment given for damages for personal injuries or death which exceed £200 subsection (1) shall have effect—

(*a*) with the substitution of "shall be included" for "may be included"; and

(*b*) with the addition of "unless the court is satisfied that there are special reasons to the contrary" after "given", where first occurring.

(3) Subject to rules of court, where—

(*a*) there are proceedings (whenever instituted) before the High Court for the recovery of a debt; and

(*b*) the defendant pays the whole debt to the plaintiff (otherwise than in pursuance of a judgment in the proceedings),

the defendant shall be liable to pay the plaintiff simple interest at such rate as the court thinks fit or as rules of court may provide on all or any part of the debt for all or any part of the period between the date when the cause of action arose and the date of the payment.

(4) Interest in respect of a debt shall not be awarded under this section for a period during which, for whatever reason, interest on the debt already runs.

(5) Without prejudice to the generality of section 84, rules of court may provide for a rate of interest by reference to the rate specified in section 17 of the Judgments Act 1838 as that section has effect from time to time or by reference to a rate for which any other enactment provides.

(6) Interest under this section may be calculated at different rates in respect of different periods.

(7) In this section "plaintiff" means the person seeking the debt or damages and "defendant" means the person from whom the plaintiff seeks the debt or damages and "personal injuries" includes any disease and any impairment of a person's physical or mental condition.

(8) Nothing in this section affects the damages recoverable for the dishonour of a bill of exchange.

PART II

SECTION INSERTED IN COUNTY COURTS ACT 1959

Interest on debts and damages

Power of county courts to award interest on debts and damages

97A.—(1) Subject to county court rules, in proceedings (whenever instituted) before a county court for the recovery of a debt or damages there may be included in any sum for which judgment is given simple interest, at such rate as the court thinks fit or as county court rules may provide, on all or any part of the debt or damages in respect of which judgment is given, or payment is made before judgment, for all or any part of the period between the date when the cause of action arose and—

(a) in the case of any sum paid before judgment, the date of the payment; and

(b) in the case of the sum for which judgment is given, the date of the judgment.

(2) In relation to a judgment given for damages for personal injuries or death which exceed £200 subsection (1) above shall have effect—

(a) with the substitution of "shall be included" for "may be included"; and

(b) with the addition of "unless the court is satisfied that there are special reasons to the contrary" after "given", where first occurring.

(3) Subject to county court rules, where—

(a) there are proceedings (whenever instituted) before a county court for the recovery of a debt; and

(b) the defendant pays the whole debt to the plaintiff (otherwise than in pursuance of a judgment in the proceedings),

the defendant shall be liable to pay the plaintiff simple interest at such rate as the court thinks fit or as county court rules may provide on all or any part of the debt for all or any part of the period between the date when the cause of action arose and the date of the payment.

(4) Interest in respect of a debt shall not be awarded under this section for a period during which, for whatever reason, interest on the debt already runs.

(5) Interest under this section may be calculated at different rates in respect of different periods.

(6) In this section "plaintiff" means the person seeking the debt or damages and "defendant" means the person from whom the plaintiff seeks the debt or damages and "personal injuries" includes any disease and any impairment of a person's physical or mental condition.

(7) Nothing in this section affects the damages recoverable for the dishonour of a bill of exchange.

(8) In determining whether an amount exceeds—

(a) the county court limit; or

(b) an amount specified in any provision of this Act,

no account shall be taken of the provisions of this section or of anything done under it.

PART III

CONSEQUENTIAL AMENDMENT OF CROWN PROCEEDINGS ACT 1947

In section 24(3) of the Crown Proceedings Act 1947 for the words from the beginning to "damages)" there shall be substituted the words "Section 35A of the Supreme Court Act 1981 and section 97A of the County Courts Act 1959 (which respectively empower the High Court and county courts to award interest on debts and damages) and section 3 of the Law Reform (Miscellaneous Provisions) Act 1934 (which empowers other courts of record to do so)".

PART IV

SECTION INSERTED IN ARBITRATION ACT 1950

Power of arbitrator to award interest
19A.—(1) Unless a contrary intention is expressed therein, every arbitration agreement shall, where such a provision is applicable to the reference, be deemed to contain a provision that the arbitrator or umpire may, if he thinks fit, award simple interest at such rate as he thinks fit—
  (*a*) on any sum which is the subject of the reference but which is paid before the award, for such period ending not later than the date of the payment as he thinks fit; and
  (*b*) on any sum which he awards, for such period ending not later than the date of the award as he thinks fit.
(2) The power to award interest conferred on an arbitrator or umpire by subsection (1) above is without prejudice to any other power of an arbitrator or umpire to award interest.

———

GENERAL NOTE
Part I
This new section (which comes into operation on January 1, 1983—s.73(11) and applies to proceedings whenever instituted is inserted in the Supreme Court Act 1981 as a result of criticisms of the existing law by the Law Commission in their Report on Interest (Report No. 88, Cmnd. 7229) and by the Court of Appeal in *Tehno-Impex* v. *Gebr van Weelde Sheepvaartkantoor BV* [1981] 1 Q.B. 648, C.A. Under the existing law (see the General Note to s.15, above), the court could award interest only on sums for which it gave judgment. If, therefore, the defendant paid to the plaintiff the whole or part of the sums before judgment, the defendant escaped having to pay interest, no matter how overdue the payment, owing to the common-law rule that interest was not payable on a debt, unless contracted for or given by statute (for example, the Bankruptcy Act 1914, s.33(8)), or arising from a particular relationship, for example executor/beneficiary or mortgagor/mortgagee. This section abolishes the common-law rule (and therefore alters the substantive commercial law as well as procedure) to the extent that the court has a discretion to award interest not only on judgment debts but also (to the date of payment) on sums paid beforehand. In both cases interest can be from the date the cause of action arose to the date of payment or judgment, though the court may allow only a shorter period. Where damages for personal injuries are concerned, the court *must* award interest unless there are special reasons to the contrary (s.35A(2), repeating a similar provision in the Administration of Justice Act 1969, s.22). The interest awarded by the Court is not to be regarded as income for income tax purposes (s.71, above).

S.35A(1)
This subsection concerns *judgments* for debts and damages (other than for personal injuries, as to which see s.35A(2) below) and gives the court a discretion to award simple interest for any period between the date the cause of action arose and the date of judgment (or earlier payment). For the rate of interest, see the note to s.35A(5), below. Where there is no judgment, because the defendant has paid the whole of a debt to the plaintiff, the court can still award interest under s.35A(3) below.

S.35A(2)

This subsection obliges the court to award interest on damages for personal injuries (defined by s.35A(7)) unless there are special reasons to the contrary (see General Note to s.35A).

S.35A(3)

See note to subs.(1) above.

S35A(4)

Only simple interest is permitted by s.35A. For circumstances in which "interest on the debt already runs," see the General Note to s.35A (above). Such interest, however low, excludes the court's power to award interest for the relevant period.

S.35A(5)

This concerns the rate of interest, which is to be fixed by rules of court (as to which, see the general rule-making power in s.84 of the Supreme Court Act 1981 and Rules of the Supreme Court, Ord. 6, r.2, Ord. 13, r.1 and Ord. 42, rr.1, 3). S.17 of the Judgments Act 1838 provides for obligatory interest on a judgment debt *from the date of judgment* at a rate which is now fixed by order (see S.I. 1980 No. 672). The court may award interest at different rates for different periods (s.35A(6)). For the rate of interest on damages for personal injuries, see *Birkett* v. *Hayes* [1982] 1 W.L.R. 817, C.A. (2 per cent. appropriate rate on general damages).

S.35A(7)

The extended definitions of "plaintiff" and "defendant" are necessary because of the provision of s.35A(3) that the court can award interest on a debt, etc., for which it does not give judgment. The definition of "personal injuries" is used in many statutes, for example s.1(6)) of the Fatal Accidents Act 1976, as substituted by s.3(1) of the present Act.

S.35A(8)

For the damages recoverable for the dishonour of a bill of exchange, see Bills of Exchange Act 1882, s.57.

Part II

This provision inserts a new s.97A into the County Courts Act 1959, which is precisely to the same effect as the new s.35A of the Supreme Court Act 1981 inserted by Pt. I of this Schedule. The note to Pt. I of this Schedule should therefore be consulted. The only differences are that there is no reference to the Judgments Act 1838, s.17 (*cf.* new s.35A(5) of the Supreme Court Act 1981) and the award of interest by a county court is not to be taken into account in determining the financial limit of the court's jurisdiction (as to which, see s.37, above).

Part III

The effect of this amendment is to apply the new s.35A of the Supreme Court Act 1981 and s.97A of the County Courts Act 1959 the provision of s.24(3) of the Crown Proceedings Act 1947 that awards of interest by the courts may be made in favour of or against the Crown.

Part IV

This provision inserts a new s.19A in the Arbitration Act 1950, which has the same effect as the new s.35A of the Supreme Court Act 1981, as to which see the note to Pt. I of this Schedule. Previously, an arbitrator had no power to award interest on his award (*Podar Trading Co.* v. *Tagher* [1949] 2 K.B. 277 and *cf. Tehno-Impex* v. *Gebr van Weelde Sheepvartkantoor BV* [1981] 1 Q.B. 648).

Section 27   SCHEDULE 2

THE ANNEX TO THE CONVENTION ON INTERNATIONAL WILLS

UNIFORM LAW ON THE FORM OF AN INTERNATIONAL WILL

ARTICLE 1

1. A will shall be valid as regards form, irrespective particularly of the place where it is made, of the location of the assets and of the nationality, domicile or residence of the

testator, if it is made in the form of an international will complying with the provisions set out in Articles 2 to 5 hereinafter.

2. The invalidity of the will as an international will shall not affect its formal validity as a will of another kind.

ARTICLE 2

This law shall not apply to the form of testamentary dispositions made by two or more persons in one instrument.

ARTICLE 3

1. The will shall be made in writing.
2. It need not be written by the testator himself.
3. It may be written in any language, by hand or by any other means.

ARTICLE 4

1. The testator shall declare in the presence of two witnesses and of a person authorized to act in connection with international wills that the document is his will and that he knows the contents thereof.
2. The testator need not inform the witnesses, or the authorized person, of the contents of the will.

ARTICLE 5

1. In the presence of the witnesses and of the authorized person, the testator shall sign the will or, if he has previously signed it, shall acknowledge his signature.
2. When the testator is unable to sign, he shall indicate the reason therefor to the authorized person who shall make note of this on the will. Moreover, the testator may be authorized by the law under which the authorized person was designated to direct another person to sign on his behalf.
3. The witnesses and the authorized person shall there and then attest the will by signing in the presence of the testator.

ARTICLE 6

1. The signatures shall be placed at the end of the will.
2. If the will consists of several sheets, each sheet shall be signed by the testator or, if he is unable to sign, by the person signing on his behalf or, if there is no such person, by the authorized person. In addition, each sheet shall be numbered.

ARTICLE 7

1. The date of the will shall be the date of its signature by the authorized person.
2. This date shall be noted at the end of the will by the authorized person.

ARTICLE 8

In the absence of any mandatory rule pertaining to the safekeeping of the will, the authorized person shall ask the testator whether he wishes to make a declaration concerning the safekeeping of his will. If so and at the express request of the testator the place where he intends to have his will kept shall be mentioned in the certificate provided for in Article 9.

ARTICLE 9

The authorized person shall attach to the will a certificate in the form prescribed in Article 10 establishing that the obligations of this law have been complied with.

ARTICLE 10

The certificate drawn up by the authorized person shall be in the following form or in a substantially similar form:

CERTIFICATE
(Convention of October 26th, 1973)

1. I, ... (name, address and capacity), a person authorized to act in connection with international wills

2. Certify that on .... (date) at ....
   .... (place)

3. (testator) .... (name, address, date and place
   of birth)
   in my presence and that of the witnesses

4. (*a*) .... (name, address, date and place of
   birth)
   (*b*) .... (name, address, date and place of
   birth)
   has declared that the attached document is his will and that he knows the contents
   thereof.

5. I furthermore certify that:

6. (*a*) in my presence and in that of the witnesses
       (1) the testator has signed the will or has acknowledged his signature previously
          affixed.
     *(2) following a declaration of the testator stating that he was unable to sign his
         will for the following reason ....
         ....
         —I have mentioned this declaration on the will
         *—the signature has been affixed by.....................(name, address)

7. (*b*) the witnesses and I have signed the will;

8. *(*c*) each page of the will has been signed by..........................and numbered:

9. (*d*) I have satisfied myself as to the identity of the testator and of the witnesses as
   designated above;

10. (*e*) the witnesses met the conditions requisite to act as such according to the law
    under which I am acting;

11. *(*f*) the testator has requested me to include the following statement concerning the
    safekeeping of his will:
    ....
    ....

12.   Place
13.   Date
14.   Signature and, if necessary, Seal
          *To be completed if appropriate.

Article II

The authorized person shall keep a copy of the certificate and deliver another to the testator.

Article 12

In the absence of evidence to the contrary, the certificate of the authorized person shall be conclusive of the formal validity of the instrument as a will under this Law.

Article 13

The absence or irregularity of a certificate shall not affect the formal validity of a will under this Law.

Article 14

The international will shall be subject to the ordinary rules of revocation of wills.

Article 15

In interpreting and applying the provisions of this law, regard shall be had to its international origin and to the need for uniformity in its interpretation.

General Note

This Schedule reproduces the Annex to the Convention providing a Uniform Law on the form of an International Will of October 26, 1973 (the UNIDROIT Convention). For the context and effect of the Annex, see the General Notes to ss.27 and 28 above.

Section 37   SCHEDULE 3

MONETARY LIMITS OF COUNTY COURT JURISDICTION

PART I

THE COUNTY COURT LIMIT

1.—(1) The following definition shall be inserted after the definition of "bailiff" in section 201 of the County Courts Act 1959—

" "the county court limit", in relation to any enactment contained in this Act, means the county court limit for the time being specified by an Order under section 192 of this Act as the county court limit for the purposes of that enactment;".

(2) Until the coming into force of the first Order under section 192 of the County Courts Act 1959 which specifies the county court limit for the purposes of any enactment the definition of "the county court limit" in sub-paragraph (1) above shall have effect in relation to that enactment as if the reference to an Order under section 192 were a reference to any Order in Council or order defining the limit of county court jurisdiction for the purposes of that enactment.

PART II

AMENDMENTS OF ENACTMENTS SPECIFYING MONETARY LIMITS

2. The words "the county court limit" shall be substituted for every reference to a sum of money in the enactments specified in paragraph 3 below.

3. The enactments mentioned in paragraph 2 above are—

(*a*) in the County Courts Act 1959—

section 39 (contract and tort)
section 40 (money recoverable by statute)
section 41 (abandonment of excess)
section 47(1) (costs of actions in High Court for small claims)
section 47(1A) (costs of actions in High Court to recover goods of small value)
section 52 (equity)
section 62 (probate)
section 68 (transfer of interpleader from High Court to county court)
section 80 (action by minor for wages)
section 102(3)(*c*) (registrars' jurisdiction)
section 146 (attachment of debts)
section 148 (administration orders)
Schedule 1 (miscellaneous jurisdiction); and

(*b*) the following provisions of other Acts—

(i) in the Settled Land Act 1925, section 113(3);
(ii) in the Consumer Credit Act 1974, section 139(5) re-opening of extortionate credit agreements);
(iii) in the Solicitors Act 1974, section 69(3) (actions for solicitors' costs);
(iv) in the Charging Orders Act 1979, section 1(2)(*c*).

4. The following subsection shall be inserted—

(*a*) after section 113(3) of the Settled Land Act 1925, as section 113(3A);
(*b*) after section 139(5) of the Consumer Credit Act 1974, as subsection (5A); and
(*c*) after section 69(3) of the Solicitors Act 1974, as section 69(4)—

"In the preceding subsection "the county court limit" means the county court limit for the time being specified by an Order in Council under section 192 of the County Courts Act 1959 as the county court limit for the purposes of that subsection.".

5.—(1) The following section shall be inserted after section 52 of the County Courts Act 1959—

"Jurisdiction under inheritance (Provision for Family and Dependants) Act 1975

52A.—(1) A county court shall have jurisdiction to hear and determine any application for an order under section 2 of the Inheritance (Provision for Family and Dependants) Act 1975 (including any application for permission to apply for such an order and any application made, in the proceedings on an application for an order under the said section 2, for an order under any other provision of that Act) where it is shown to the satisfaction of the court that the value at the date of the death of the deceased of all property included in his net estate for the purposes of that Act by virtue of paragraph (*a*) of the definition of "net estate" in section 25(1) of that Act does not exceed the county court limit.

(2) In the preceding subsection "the county court limit" means the county court limit for the time being specified by an Order in Council under section 192 of the County Courts Act 1959 as the county court limit for the purposes of that subsection."

(2) In section 53(2) of that Act (jurisdiction by agreement) for the words "the last foregoing section" there shall be substituted the words "either of the two foregoing sections".

6. In section 1(2) of the Charging Orders Act 1979, after the word "section", in the first place where it occurs, there shall be inserted the words ""county court limit" means the county court limit for the time being specified in an Order in Council under section 192 of the County Courts Act 1959, as the county court limit for the purposes of this section and".

PART III

POWER TO RAISE COUNTY COURT LIMIT

7. The following section shall be substituted for section 192 of the County Courts Act 1959—

"Power of Her Majesty to raise limits of jurisdiction of courts

192.—(1) If it appears to Her Majesty in Council that the county court limit for the purposes of any enactment referring to that limit should be increased, Her Majesty may by Order in Council direct that the county court limit for the purposes of that enactment shall be such sum as may be specified in the Order.

(2) An Order under subsection (1) of this section may contain such incidental or transitional provisions as Her Majesty considers appropriate.

(3) No recommendation shall be made to Her Majesty in Council to make an Order under this section unless a draft of the Order has been laid before Parliament and approved by resolution of each House of Parliament.".

PART IV

HIGHWAYS

8.—(1) Sums recoverable under section 59 of the Highways Act 1980 (expenses due to extraordinary traffic) shall be recoverable in the county court if the claim does not exceed the county court limit for the purposes of section 40 of the County Courts Act 1959 (general jurisdiction as to money recoverable by statute).

(2) In subsection (4) of that section, for the words from the beginning to "in" in the second place where it occurs, there shall be substituted the words "The county court with jurisdiction to hear and determine a claim for a sum recoverable under this section is".

GENERAL NOTE

For the general purpose of this Schedule, see the General Note to s.37, above. All of the amendments are for this purpose, *i.e.* making uniform references to "the county court limit" in the many enactments which hitherto had referred to specific financial limits. The reference in para. 5 to a new s.52A of the County Courts Act 1959 merely replaces in effect s.22 of the Inheritance (Provision for Family and Dependants) Act 1975, which is repealed by s.72 and Sched. 9 of the present Act. The new s.192 of the County Courts Act 1959, substituted by Pt. III of this Schedule, gives a general power to raise the "county court limit" (defined in para. 1 of this Schedule) for all the enactments that, by virtue of this Schedule, now use that phrase.

Section 55   SCHEDULE 4

ATTACHMENT OF DEBTS

PART I

SECTION INSERTED IN SUPREME COURT ACT 1981

Administrative and clerical expenses of garnishees

40A.—(1) A sum may be prescribed which, before complying with an order made in the exercise of the jurisdiction mentioned in section 40(2)—

(*a*) any deposit-taking institution; or

(*b*) any such institution of a prescribed description,

may deduct, subject to subsection (2) below, towards the clerical and administrative expenses of complying with the order, from any money which, but for the deduction, would be attached by the order.

(2) The prescribed sum may not be deducted or, as the case may be, retained in a case where, by virtue of section 40 of the Bankruptcy Act 1914 or section 325 of the Companies Act 1948 or otherwise, the creditor is not entitled to retain the benefit of the attachment.

(3) In this section—

"deposit-taking institution" has the meaning assigned to it by section 40(6); and

"prescribed" means prescribed by an order made by the Lord Chancellor.

(4) An order under this section—

(*a*) may make different provision for different cases; and

(*b*) without prejudice to the generality of paragraph (*a*) of this subsection, may prescribe sums differing according to the amount due under the judgment or order to be satisfied.

(5) Any such order shall be made by statutory instrument subject to annulment in pursuance of a resolution of either House of Parliament.

PART II

SECTION INSERTED IN COUNTY COURTS ACT 1959

Administrative and clerical expenses of garnishees

143A.—(1) A sum may be prescribed which, before complying with an order made in the exercise of the jurisdiction mentioned in section 143(2) of this Act—

(*a*) any deposit-taking institution; or

(*b*) any such institution of a prescribed description,

may deduct, subject to subsection (2) below, towards the clerical and administrative expenses of complying with the order, from any money which, but for the deduction, would be attached by the order.

(2) The prescribed sum may not be deducted or, as the case may be, retained in a case where, by virtue of section 40 of the Bankruptcy Act 1914 or section 325 of the Companies Act 1948 or otherwise, the creditor is not entitled to retain the benefit of the attachment.

(3) In this section—

"deposit-taking institution" has the meaning assigned to it by section 143(6) of this Act; and

"prescribed" means prescribed by an order made by the Lord Chancellor.

(4) An order under this section—

(*a*) may make different provision for different cases; and

(*b*) without prejudice to the generality of paragraph (*a*) of this subsection, may prescribe sums differing according to the amount due under the judgment or order to be satisfied.

(5) Any such order shall be made by statutory instrument subject to annulment in pursuance of a resolution of either House of Parliament.

GENERAL NOTE

For an explanation of the effect of this Schedule, see the General Note to s.55, above.

Section 67   SCHEDULE 5

LAND REGISTRATION

In the Land Registration Act 1925—

   (*a*) the following paragraph shall be substituted for section 3(ii)—

     ""(ii) "the court" means the High Court or, where county courts have jurisdiction by virtue of rules made under section 138(1) of this Act, the county court;";

   (*b*) the following section shall be substituted for section 112—

"Inspection of register and other documents at Land Registry

   112.—(1) Subject—

     (*a*) to section 112A below;

     (*b*) to the provisions of this Act as to furnishing information to Government departments and local authorities; and

     (*c*) to such exceptions as may be prescribed,

any person registered as proprietor of any land or charge, and any person authorised—

     (i) by any such proprietor; or

     (ii) by an order made under subsection (2) or (3) of this section; or

     (iii) by general rule,

but no other person, shall have a right, on payment of a fee and in accordance with the prescribed procedure, to inspect and make copies of the whole or any part of any register or document in the custody of the register relating to such land or charge.

   (2) The High Court may by order authorise—

     (*a*) the inspection of a register or document in the custody of the registrar and relating to land or a charge; and

     (*b*) the making of copies of the whole or any part of any such register or document,

   if—

     (i) it appears to the court that the register or any such document may contain information which is relevant to proceedings pending in the court (including proceedings for the enforcement of a judgment or order of the High Court or any other court); or

     (ii) it appears to the court, on an application made for that purpose, that such an order ought to be made for any other reason.

   (3) A county court may by order authorise—

     (*a*) the inspection of a register or document in the custody of the registrar and relating to land or a charge; and

     (*b*) the making of copies of the whole or any part of any such register or document,

if it appears to the court that the register or any such document may contain information which is relevant to proceedings pending in the court (including proceedings for the enforcement of a judgment or order of the court or of any other court).";

   (*c*) the following section shall be substituted for section 138—

"Jurisdiction of High Court and county courts

   138.—(1) Any jurisdiction conferred on the High Court by this Act or by the Land Registration and Land Charges Act 1971 may also be exercised, to such extent as may be prescribed, by county courts.

   (2) Subject to the enactments relating to the Supreme Court of Judicature for the time being in force, all matters within the jurisdiction

of the High Court under this Act or the said Act of 1971 shall be assigned to the Chancery Division of that court.

(3) Where the county court has jurisdiction under this Act or that Act it shall have all the powers of the High Court for the purposes of that jurisdiction.

(4) The Lord Chancellor may assign any duties of the High Court under this Act or that Act to any particular judge or judges of the High Court."; and

(*d*) in section 144(1) (which among other things provides for the inclusion in the Rule Committee of a judge of the Chancery Division chosen by the judges of that division) for the words "to be chosen by the judges of that division" there shall be substituted the words "nominated by the Lord Chancellor".

GENERAL NOTE
See the General Note to s.67 (above).

Section 68   SCHEDULE 6

DAMAGES FOR PERSONAL INJURIES, ETC.—NORTHERN IRELAND

Abolition of actions for enticement, seduction and harbouring of child

1. No person shall be liable in tort under the law of Northern Ireland—
    (*a*) to a parent (or person standing in the place of a parent) on the ground only of his having deprived the parent (or other person) of the services of his or her child by raping, seducing or enticing that child; or
    (*b*) to any other person for harbouring the child of that other person.

Fatal accidents

2. The following paragraph shall be substituted for paragraph (2) of Article 2 of the Fatal Accidents (Northern Ireland) Order 1977—

"(2) In this Order "dependant" means—
    (*a*) the wife or husband or former wife or husband of the deceased;
    (*b*) any person who—
        (i) was living with the deceased in the same household immediately before the date of the death; and
        (ii) had been living with the deceased in the same household for at least two years before that date; and
        (iii) was living during the whole of that period as the husband or wife of the deceased;
    (*c*) any parent or other ascendant of the deceased;
    (*d*) any person who was treated by the deceased as his parent;
    (*e*) a child or other descendant of the deceased;
    (*f*) any person (not being a child of the deceased) who, in the case of any marriage to which the deceased was at any time a party, was treated by the deceased as a child of the family in relation to that marriage;
    (*g*) any person who is, or is the issue of, a brother, sister, uncle or aunt of the deceased;
and "the deceased" has the meaning given by Article 3(2).

(2A) The reference to the former wife or husband of the deceased in paragraph (2)(*a*) includes a reference to a person whose marriage to the deceased has been annulled or declared void as well as a person whose marriage to the deceased has been dissolved.".

3. In paragraph (2) of Article 3 of that Order for the word "Every" there shall be substituted the words "Subject to Article 3A(2), every".

4. The following shall be inserted after that Article—

"*Bereavement*

3A.—(1) An action under this Order may consist of or include a claim for damages for bereavement.

(2) A claim for damages for bereavement shall only be for the benefit—

    (*a*) of the wife or husband of the deceased; and
    (*b*) where the deceased was a minor who was never married—
        (i) of his parents, if he was legitimate; and
        (ii) of his mother, if he was illegitimate.

    (3) Subject to paragraph (5), the sum to be awarded as damages under this Article shall be £3,500.

    (4) Where the claim is a claim for damages under this Article for the benefit of both the parents of the deceased, the sum awarded shall be divided equally between them (subject to any deduction falling to be made in respect of costs not recovered from the defendant).

    (5) The Lord Chancellor may by order made by statutory instrument, subject to annulment in pursuance of a resolution of either House of Parliament, amend this Article by varying the sum for the time being specified in paragraph (3).".

   5. In Article 4 of that Order—
    (*a*) in paragraph (2), for the word "dependants" there shall be substituted the words "persons for whose benefit an executor or administrator could have brought it"; and
    (*b*) in paragraph (4), for the word "dependants" there shall be substituted the word "persons".

   6.—(1) The following paragraphs shall be substituted for paragraph (1) of Article 5—
    "(1) In the action such damages, other than damages for bereavement, may be awarded as are proportioned to the injury resulting from the death to the dependants respectively.

    (1A) After deducting the costs not recovered from the defendant any amount recovered otherwise than as damages for bereavement shall be divided among the dependants in such shares as may be directed.".

    (2) In paragraph (2), for "(1)" there shall be substituted "(1A)".

    (3) In paragraph (3), for the words "In assessing damages payable to a widow in respect of the death of her husband in an action under this Order" there shall be substituted the words "In an action under this Order where there fall to be assessed damages payable to a widow in respect of the death of her husband".

    (4) The following paragraph shall be inserted after that paragraph—
    "(3A) In an action under this Order where there fall to be assessed damages payable to a person who is a dependant by virtue of Article 2(2)(*b*) in respect of the death of the person with whom the dependant was living as husband or wife there shall be taken into account (together with any other matter that appears to the court to be relevant to the action) the fact that the dependant had no enforceable right to financial support by the deceased as a result of their living together.".

    (5) In paragraph (5), for the words "the dependants' shares" there shall be substituted the words "any person's share".

   7. The following shall be substituted for Article 6—
    "*Assessment of damages: disregard of benefits*
      6.—(1) In assessing damages in respect of a person's death in an action under this Order, benefits which have accrued or will or may accrue to any person from his estate or otherwise as a result of his death shall be disregarded.".

   8. In Article 7, the words "brought for the benefit of the dependants of that person" shall be omitted.

Exclusion of section 14 of Law Reform (Miscellaneous Provisions) Act (Northern Ireland) 1937

   9.—(1) The following subsection shall be inserted after section 14(1) of the Law Reform (Miscellaneous Provisions) Act (Northern Ireland) 1937 (actions to survive death)—
    "(1A) The right of a person to claim under Article 3A of the Fatal Accidents (Northern Ireland) Order 1977 (bereavement) shall not survive for the benefit of his estate on his death.".

    (2) The following paragraph shall be substituted for subsection (2)(*a*)—
    "(*a*) shall not include—
        (i) any exemplary damages;
        (ii) any damages for loss of income in respect of any period after that person's death;".

Orders for provisional damages for personal injury

   10.—(1) This paragraph applies to an action under the law of Northern Ireland for damages for personal injuries in which there is proved or admitted to be a chance that at some definite or indefinite time in the future the injured person will, as a result of the act or omission which gave rise to the cause of action, develop some serious disease or suffer some serious deterioration in his physical or mental condition.

(2) Subject to sub-paragraph (4) below, as regards any action for damages to which this paragraph applies in which a judgment is given in the High Court, provision may be made by rules of court for enabling the court, in such circumstances as may be prescribed, to award the injured person—

(*a*) damages assessed on the assumption that the injured person will not develop the disease or suffer deterioration in his condition; and

(*b*) further damages at a future date if he develops the disease or suffers the deterioration.

(3) Any rules made by virtue of this paragraph may include such incidental, supplementary and consequential provisions as the rule-making authority may consider necessary or expedient.

(4) Nothing in this paragraph shall be construed—

(*a*) as affecting the exercise of any power relating to costs, including any power to make rules of court relating to costs; or

(*b*) as prejudicing any duty of the court under any enactment or rule of law to reduce or limit the total damages which would have been recoverable apart from any such duty.

(5) This paragraph shall have effect in relation to county courts in Northern Ireland as it has effect in relation to the High Court as if references in it to rules of court included references to county court rules.

(6) In this paragraph "personal injuries" includes any disease and any impairment of a person's physical or mental condition.

GENERAL NOTE

The General Note to s.68 above should be consulted for references to the effect of this Schedule.

Section 69   SCHEDULE 7

INTEREST ON DEBTS AND DAMAGES—NORTHERN IRELAND

PART I

SECTION INSERTED IN JUDICATURE (NORTHERN IRELAND) ACT 1978

Power of High Court to award interest on debts and damages

33A.—(1) Subject to rules of court, in proceedings (whenever instituted) before the High Court for the recovery of a debt or damages there may be included in any sum for which judgment is given simple interest, at such rate as the court thinks fit or as rules of court may provide, on all or any part of the debt or damages in respect of which judgment is given, or payment is made before judgment, for all or any part of the period between the date when the cause of action arose and—

(i) in the case of any sum paid before judgment, the date of the payment; and

(ii) in the case of the sum for which judgment is given, the date of the judgment.

(2) Subject to the rules of court, where—

(*a*) there are proceedings (whenever instituted) before the High Court for the recovery of a debt; and

(*b*) the defendant pays the whole debt to the plaintiff (otherwise than in pursuance of a judgment in the proceedings),

the defendant shall be liable to pay the plaintiff simple interest at such rate as the court thinks fit or as rules of court may provide on all or any part of the debt for all or any part of the period between the date when the cause of action arose and the date of the payment.

(3) Interest in respect of a debt shall not be awarded under this section for a period during which, for whatever reason, interest on the debt already runs.

(4) Without prejudice to the generality of section 55, rules of court may provide for a rate of interest by reference to a rate for which any other enactment provides.

(5) Interest under this section may be calculated at different rates in respect of different periods.

(6) In this section "plaintiff" means the person seeking the debt or damages and "defendant" means the person from whom the plaintiff seeks the debt or damages.

(7) Nothing in this section affects the damages recoverable for the dishonour of a bill of exchange.

PART II

ARTICLE INSERTED IN COUNTY COURTS (NORTHERN IRELAND) ORDER 1980

Interest on debts and damages

45A.—(1) Subject to county court rules, in proceedings (whenever instituted) before a county court for the recovery of a debt or damages there may be included in any sum for which judgment is given simple interest, at such rate as the court thinks fit or as county court rules may provide, on all or any part of the debt or damages in respect of which judgment is given, or payment is made before judgment, for all or any part of the period between the date when the cause of action arose and—

  (i) in the case of any sum paid before judgment, the date of the payment; and

  (ii) in the case of the sum for which judgment is given, the date of the judgment.

(2) Subject to county court rules, where—

    (*a*) there are proceedings (whenever instituted) before a county court for the recovery of a debt; and

    (*b*) the defendant pays the whole debt to the plaintiff (otherwise than in pursuance of a judgment in the proceedings),

the defendant shall be liable to pay the plaintiff simple interest at such rate as the court thinks fit or as county court rules may provide on all or any part of the debt for all or any part of the period between the date when the cause of action arose and the date of the payment.

(3) Interest in respect of a debt shall not be awarded under this Article for a period during which, for whatever reason, interest on the debt already runs.

(4) Interest under this Article may be calculated at different rates in respect of different periods.

(5) In this Article "plaintiff" means the person seeking the debt or damages and "defendant" means the person from whom the plaintiff seeks the debt or damage.

(6) Nothing in this Article affects the damages recoverable for the dishonour of a bill of exchange.

PART III

AMENDMENTS CONSEQUENTIAL ON SECTION 69

Crown Proceedings Act 1947 (c. 44)

1. In section 24(3) of the Crown Proceedings Act 1947 as it applies in Northern Ireland in relation to Her Majesty's Government in the United Kingdom and in relation to Her Majesty's Government in Northern Ireland for the words from the beginning to "damages)" there shall be substituted the words "Section 33A of the Judicature (Northern Ireland) Act 1978 and Article 45A of the County Courts (Northern Ireland) Order 1980 (which respectively empower the High Court and county courts to award interest on debts and damages)".

Judicature (Northern Ireland) Act 1978 (c. 23)

2. In section 31(9)(*c*) of the Judicature (Northern Ireland) Act 1978 for the words "section 17 of the Law Reform (Miscellaneous Provisions) Act (Northern Ireland) 1937" there shall be substituted the words "Article 45A of the County Courts (Northern Ireland) Order 1980".

County Courts (Northern Ireland) Order 1980

3. In Article 2(4) of the County Courts (Northern Ireland) Order 1980 for the words from "the power" to the end there shall be substituted the words "Article 45A or of anything done under it".

GENERAL NOTE

The General Note to s.69 above should be consulted for references to the effect of this Schedule.

Section 70   SCHEDULE 8

AMENDMENTS OF JUDICATURE (NORTHERN IRELAND) ACT 1978

1. The following subsection shall be added at the end of section 3 (the Court of Appeal)—

"(6) Her Majesty may by Order in Council from time to time create divisions or additional divisions of the Court of Appeal or provide that any division be abolished; and any such Order in Council may contain such provision as may appear to Her Majesty to be necessary or proper for that purpose and may amend or repeal any statutory provision (including any provision of this Act) so far as it appears to Her Majesty to be necessary or expedient to do so in consequence of the Order.".

2. In section 13 (which among other things provides for the taking of the oath of allegiance and the judicial oath by judges of the Supreme Court of Judicature of Northern Ireland)—

(a) in subsection (2) (which requires the Lord Chief Justice, every Lord Justice of Appeal and every judge of the High Court to take the oaths in the presence of the Lord Chancellor) the words "every Lord Justice of Appeal and every judge of the High Court" shall cease to have effect; and

(b) the following subsections shall be added after subsection (3)—

"(4) Subject to subsection (5), every Lord Justice of Appeal and every judge of the High Court shall, before he enters on the execution of his office, take, in the presence of the Lord Chancellor, the oaths mentioned in subsection (2).

(5) When the Lord Chancellor so directs or the Great Seal of the United Kingdom is in commission, the Lord Chief Justice shall represent the Lord Chancellor for the purposes of subsection (4).".

3. In section 27(1)(b) (which empowers the High Court in Northern Ireland to make an order requiring parents of a ward of court to make periodical payments towards the maintenance and education of the ward) after the words "the ward" there shall be inserted the words "or to the ward".

4. In subsection (3) of section 53 (which applies to certain provisions relating to the Supreme Court Rules Committee to the Crown Court Rules Committee and the Crown Court rules) for the words "56(1) and (2)" there shall be substituted the words "56(1), (2) and (2A)".

5. The following subsection shall be inserted after subsection (2) of section 56 (control and publication of rules of court)—

"(2A) Rules made by the Rules Committee shall be statutory rules for the purposes of the Statutory Rules (Northern Ireland) Order 1979.".

6. In section 78(1)(a) (accounts of funds in court) for the words "Part I of the Administration of Justice Act 1965" there shall be substituted the words "Part VI of the Administration of Justice Act 1982".

7. In section 81(a)(ii) (which provides for the investment of funds in court) for the words "section 1 of the Administration of Justice Act 1965" there shall be substituted the words "section 42 of the Administration of Justice Act 1982".

8. In section 82(1) (rules regulating funds in court)—

(a) in paragraph (b)(ii), for the words "section 1 of the Administration of Justice Act 1965" there shall be substituted the words "section 42 of the Administration of Justice Act 1982"; and

(b) in paragraph (d) for the words "section 1 of the Administration of Justice Act 1965" there shall be substituted the words "section 42 of the Administration of Justice Act 1982"; and

(c) in paragraph (i) for the words "the Public Trustee" there shall be substituted the words "the investment manager of a common investment scheme made under section 42 of the Administration of Justice Act 1982".

9. In section 85 (which provides for any default of a member of the Northern Ireland Court Service with respect to money, securities or effects in the Supreme Court or the county court or any statutory deposit to be made good by the Lord Chancellor) after the words "Lord Chancellor" there shall be added the words "or, if and so far as it is not so paid, shall be charged on and issued out of the Consolidated Fund.".

10. In section 91 (orders for sale, grant of injunctions and appointment of receivers by the High Court and county courts)—
 (*a*) in subsection (1) for the word "or", in the third place where it occurs, there shall be substituted the word "and"; and
 (*b*) the following subsection shall be added after subsection (3)—

> "(4) The power of the High Court and, in matters within its jurisdiction, the county court, to grant an interlocutory injunction restraining a party to any proceedings from removing from the jurisdiction, or otherwise dealing with, assets located within the jurisdiction shall be exercisable in cases where that party is, as well as in cases where he is not, domiciled, resident or present within the jurisdiction.".

11. The following section shall be inserted after section 94—

"Withdrawal of privilege against incrimination of self or spouse in certain proceedings
 94A.—(1) In any proceedings to which this subsection applies a person shall not be excused, by reason that to do so would tend to expose that person, or his or her spouse, to proceedings for a related offence or for the recovery of a related penalty—
 (*a*) from answering any question put to that person in the first-mentioned proceedings; or
 (*b*) from complying with any order made in those proceedings.
 (2) Subsection (1) applies to the following civil proceedings in the High Court, namely—
 (*a*) proceedings for infringement of rights pertaining to any intellectual property or for passing off;
 (*b*) proceedings brought to obtain disclosure of information relating to any infringement of such rights or to any passing off; and
 (*c*) proceedings brought to prevent any apprehended infringement of such rights or any apprehended passing off.
 (3) Subject to subsection (4), no statement or admission made by a person—
> (*a*) in answering a question put to him in any proceedings to which subsection (1) applies; or
> (*b*) in complying with any order made in any such proceedings,

shall, in proceedings for any related offence or for the recovery of any related penalty, be admissible in evidence against that person or (unless they married after the making of the statement or admission) against the spouse of that person.
 (4) Nothing in subsection (3) shall render any statement or admission made by a person as there mentioned inadmissible in evidence against that person in proceedings for perjury or contempt of court.
 (5) In this section—
> "intellectual property" means any patent, trade mark, copyright, registered design, technical or commercial information or other intellectual property;
> "related offence", in relation to any proceedings to which subsection (1) applies, means—
>> (*a*) in the case of proceedings within subsection (2)(*a*) or (*b*)—
>>> (i) any offence committed by or in the course of the infringement or passing off to which those proceedings relate; or
>>> (ii) any offence not within sub-paragraph (i) committed in connection with that infringement or passing off, being an offence involving fraud or dishonesty;
>> (*b*) in the case of proceedings within subsection (2)(*c*), any offence revealed by the facts on which the plaintiff relies in those proceedings;
> "related penalty", in relation to any proceedings to which subsection (1) applies, means—
>> (*a*) in the case of proceedings within subsection (2)(*a*) or (*b*), any penalty incurred in respect of anything done or omitted in

connection with the infringement or passing off to which those proceedings relate;

(*b*) in the case of proceedings within subsection (2)(*c*) any penalty incurred in respect of any act or omission revealed by the facts on which the plaintiff relies in those proceedings.

(6) Any reference in this section to civil proceedings in the High Court of any description includes a reference to proceedings on appeal arising out of civil proceedings in the High Court of that description.".

12. The following section shall be inserted after section 117—

"Allowances for judges

117A. The Lord Chancellor shall pay to any judge of the Court of Appeal or of the High Court, in addition to his salary, such allowances as may be determined by the Lord Chancellor with the concurrence of the Treasury.".

GENERAL NOTE

The General Note to s.70 above should be consulted for references to the effect of this Schedule.

Section 75   SCHEDULE 9

REPEALS AND REVOCATIONS

PART I

REPEALS

Chapter	Short title	Extent of repeal
15 & 16 Vict. c. 24.	Wills Act Amendment Act 1852.	The whole Act.
23 & 24 Vict. c. 115.	Crown Debts and Judgments Act 1860.	The whole Act.
59 & 60 Vict. c. 35.	Judicial Trustees Act 1896.	In section 1(6), the words from the beginning to "and", in the second place where it occurs.
4 & 5 Geo. 5. c. 59.	Bankruptcy Act 1914.	In section 16(13) and in section 28(1)(*c*), the words "under a judgment against him in an action for seduction, or".
15 & 16 Geo. 5. c. 20.	Law of Property Act 1925.	Section 177.
24 & 25 Geo. 5. c. 41.	Law Reform (Miscellaneous Provisions) Act 1934.	In section 1(1), the words "or seduction".
1 Edw. 8 & 1 Geo. 6. c. 9 (N.I.).	Law Reform (Miscellaneous Provisions) Act (Northern Ireland) 1937.	In section 14(1), the words "or seduction". Section 17.
6 & 7 Eliz. 2. c. 45.	Prevention of Fraud (Investments) Act 1958.	Section 4(3).

Chapter	Short title	Extent of repeal
7 & 8 Eliz. 2. c. 22.	County Courts Act 1959.	Section 2. Section 20. Section 25. Section 99(3). Section 102(3)(*e*). In section 148, in subsection (1)(*a*), the words "in a county court" and subsection (2). Sections 168 to 174. Section 174A. Section 176.
7 & 8 Eliz. 2. c. 72.	Mental Health Act 1959.	In section 103(1)(*h*), the words from "so however" to the end of the paragraph.
1965 c. 2.	Administration of Justice Act 1965.	Sections 1 to 16. Section 18. In section 20, subsections (1) and (2), and in subsection (7), the words from "and" to the end. In Schedule 1, the entry relating to the Prevention of Fraud (Investments) Act 1958.
1969 c. 46.	Family Law Reform Act 1969.	Section 16.
1969 c. 58.	Administration of Justice Act 1969.	Section 10.
1974 c. 4.	Legal Aid Act 1974.	In Part II of Schedule 1, paragraph 2.
1975 c. 63.	Inheritance (Provision for Family and Dependants) Act 1975.	Section 22.
1976 c. 13.	Damages (Scotland) Act 1976.	Section 5.
1976 c. 30.	Fatal Accidents Act 1976.	In section 5, the words "brought for the benefit of the dependants of that person". In Schedule 1, in paragraph 2(2) the entry relating to the Deposit of Poisonous Waste Act 1972.
1977 c. 38.	Administration of Justice Act 1977.	Section 11.
1978 c. 23.	Judicature (Northern Ireland) Act 1978.	Section 83.
1979 c. 2.	Customs and Excise Management Act 1979.	In Schedule 4, in the Table to paragraph 12, the entry relating to the Crown Debts and Judgments Act 1860.
1981 c. 54.	Supreme Court Act 1981.	Section 126. Section 143. In Schedule 3, paragraphs 23 to 26. In Schedule 5, the paragraphs relating to the Bankruptcy Act 1914 and the Companies Act 1948.

PART II

REVOCATIONS

Reference	Title	Extent of revocation
S.I. 1967 No. 761.	Land Registration Rules 1967.	The whole instrument.
S.I. 1977 No. 1251 (N.I. 18).	Fatal Accidents (Northern Ireland) Order 1977.	In Article 7, the words "brought for the benefit of the dependants of that person".
S.I. 1979 No. 1575 (N.I. 14).	Administration of Estates (Northern Ireland) Order 1979.	Article 27.

GENERAL NOTE

Reference should be made to the General Note to s.75 (above).